ARTIFICIAL INTELLIGENCE

A PRACTICAL GUIDE TO USING AI IN EVERYDAY LIFE

MATT GREENWOOD

TABLE OF CONTENTS

PREFACE

Artificial intelligence, or AI, is the long-anticipated future technology that has already arrived and has found its way into the fabric of our everyday lives. This book is here to demystify how AI works beyond the 'robots taking over the world' narrative or sci-fi movie tropes. These tropes may be fun to explore in fiction, and their underlying themes are more relevant than ever, but it's also obligatory to explore AI with a more nuanced approach.

After all, artificial intelligence has quietly made its way from science fiction into reality. It's here, and it's making life easier, more interesting, and perhaps more like those futuristic movies than we ever thought possible. As a result, humanity is left to ponder its implications as a force for good, a bringer of progress, and a potential ethical concern if misused.

Its presence is much more down-to-earth and perhaps more mundane than you might expect. There are so many applications of AI that make it an instantly appealing addition to everyday life. From waking up to an alarm that knows exactly when you're in your lightest sleep phase to getting traffic updates from a friendly voice in your car that might know the roads better than you do, AI is the invisible helper that's become a big part of what makes the world tick.

These examples are just scratching the surface. This book looks into the practical applications of AI in daily life and the way it impacts everyone's lives, both directly and indirectly. AI is already used in those smart suggestions you get while shopping online, in your phone camera when it turns a simple snapshot into a masterpiece, and in your social media feeds when they seem to know exactly what content will make you laugh, sigh, or click. The intent here is to unpack all this in a way that's as easy to understand as scrolling through your favorite social media feed. Whether you're completely new to AI or curious about how much deeper AI is integrated beyond voice commands, this might just be a piece for you. Hopefully, it will help you think of artificial intelligence as less like a distant dream and more like a companion that makes your life a tad bit smoother.

AI is behind an impressive number of technological systems, keeping everything running without a hitch while users remain blissfully unaware of the complex processes happening behind the scenes. It's the personal assistant you didn't know you had, working without a pause to make your digital life as seamless as flipping through a magazine.

However, it doesn't stop at those small conveniences that make everyday technology ostensibly 'smarter.' AI is also opening doors to new ways of learning, connecting, and taking care of health. Have you ever been curious about how your fitness app predicts your workout routine or how language learning apps seem to know exactly where you struggle? All of that is AI adjusting its numbers behind the scenes to fit your experiences. It's transforming the way we interact with the world around us, making technology more intuitive, responsive, and, dare we say, more human. That might be a slightly ironic or bold statement, but it will become clearer as you learn more about neural networks and natural language processing—more on that later. Think of this exploration of AI in daily life as discovering a new lens to view the ordinary things around you—a lens that reveals a layer of intelligence and creativity powering the modern world.

The heart of AI's impact is nothing short of a historical precedent. It's not just another tech trend. It's a revolution reshaping everything from gadgets to work, learning, and even the creation of art. It's at least as revolutionary as the invention and popularization of the Internet, but if taken far enough, it could even be comparable to various technologies that powered industrial revolutions. Of course, AI has transformed the tech landscape first—it's behind self-driving cars that could one day make traffic jams and accidents history, for example.

This technology isn't any less impactful than other major advances, economically speaking. It's optimizing everything from supply chains to energy consumption, making businesses smarter and more sustainable. It's creating jobs that never existed before, like AI ethics officers and machine learning engineers. However, it's also raising burning questions about job security, human labor, the value of labor, and the meaning of creativity and art. It reopens old questions and forces humanity into engaging with economic, social, and philosophical questions as the possibility of absolute automation becomes realistically plausible.

And let's not forget the culture shift. AI is influencing what people watch, listen to, and how they socialize online. It affects human psychology and the nature of interaction and raises some interesting questions about ethics in culture.

Now, for a taste of groundbreaking AI, consider AlphaGo, an AI that beat the world champion in Go, a game so complex it was believed to be beyond machines. Or OpenAI's GPT, which can write essays, poems, marketing copy, code, and much more. It shows the creative potential of AI. These are milestones showing AI's potential to tackle complex problems, stir up creativity, and enhance human capabilities and efficiency. Peeling back the layers of AI's influence, there's a clear necessity to envision a future where AI and humans collaborate rather than compete. It's necessary to create a world that's more efficient, creative, and inclusive without losing sight of the limitations of both humans and artificial neural networks.

If we look into AI's impact on the economy, we can see that it's reshaping industries and job landscapes. Let's envision factories where AI and humans work side by side, boosting production while cutting down waste and accidents. It's worth noting that current AI isn't broadly integrated into physical robots, so don't expect factories run by intelligent robots any time soon. Meanwhile, in agriculture, AI-powered drones and sensors are making farming more precise and less resource-intensive, helping feed a growing global population more sustainably.

Culturally, AI is the new Renaissance as it sparks a fusion of art, science, and technology. It's enabling creators to explore new horizons, from AI-composed symphonies to digital art that blurs the lines between the virtual and the real. On social media, AI algorithms are curating feeds and helping fight misinformation, at least within the scope of what's possible in light of both human and AI bias (which will also be explored). These examples underline AI's role as both a tool and a transformational force, influencing how humans live, work, and interact in a deeply interconnected world.

This book will show you all of this and more without excess technicalities. If you have little to no background in technology, you shouldn't feel lost. We will begin with the ABCs of AI, where you'll learn what AI really means beyond the media hype. You'll get to know neural networks that mimic the brain's workings and algorithms that predict the next click. The book will also explore how AI has found its way into everyday lives almost unnoticeably but rather profoundly.

However, as hinted, it is not all rosy. The book won't shy away from tackling the thorny issues, too. For one, privacy concerns with AI knowing more about you than your friends or family, or the ethical dilemmas of self-driving cars making split-second decisions. AI's impact on jobs is also complex—some will change, perhaps even disappear, but new ones will sprout up, too.

We will speculate on where AI might take the world next. Could AI help us solve the climate crisis or bring about a new era in medicine? Finally, we'll arm you with knowledge on how to coexist with AI, making you ready not just to live alongside AI but to thrive.

Being ready is immensely significant because you should expect to encounter AI in places you'd least expect—like in the art studio, where AI becomes the modern Picasso, or in the music studio, composing the next major hits. These are also aspects where artificial intelligence is most misunderstood. It's that misunderstanding that makes it particularly important to decode how AI is flipping the script in creativity and similar applications beyond crunching numbers.

Because AI works best as a team player, this reading material will showcase its role in boosting teamwork and productivity with virtual assistants that manage your calendar and business strategist AI tools.

All of this leads to the broader questions of AI ethics and bias and the general application of these subjects. Ethics are an important consideration because as smart as AI is, it's not immune to picking up our human flaws, serving as a mirror of sorts. You'll get the lowdown on how the smartest minds are working to make AI as fair and unbiased as possible, as well as all the challenges that come with it. By the end, you'll grasp the ins and outs of AI and understand its challenges and the collective efforts to steer it toward a future that benefits all.

CHAPTER 1

INTRODUCTION TO ARTIFICIAL INTELLIGENCE

Ever since generative artificial intelligence tools like ChatGPT launched in late 2022, there has been significant hype around artificial intelligence. Yet, something not everyone might know is that AI has been around long before the current AI buzz.

Virtual assistants—Siri, Alexa, and Google Assistant, to name a few, certainly aren't as sophisticated as generative AI. However, they are its clear precursors and are therefore known as 'proto-AI.' Have you ever thought about how Siri knows exactly what song you're humming or how Google Assistant somehow understands your craving for pizza on a Friday night? That's AI in action.

Social media is another great example of early AI implementation. If you've ever used Facebook or Instagram, think about how your face gets recognized when you are automatically tagged in a photo. Facial recognition has been around for over a decade, impressing many social media users and spooking others. These are just some examples of how AI has been around for years, quietly operating in the background, optimizing, assisting, and learning.

However, the apparent omnipresence of AI in the current digital space begs the question: What exactly is AI?

DEFINITION: WHAT EXACTLY IS AI?

Put simply, artificial intelligence is the simulation of human intelligence in machines. AI programs are designed to think like humans and mimic their actions. They can learn from data, make decisions, and perform tasks such as visual perception, speech recognition, decision-making, and language translation.

Even before the current iteration of AI, there have been tools and software that could simulate some of its capabilities. For example, simple chatbots could respond to messages in a way that seemingly made sense. That was until you'd say something a bit too complicated or outside of the scope of its programming.

So, how do these tools differ from 'true' AI? Think of the old chatbots as parrots. They are good at repeating a few pre-programmed words and sentences but without understanding them or coming up with anything entirely new. On the other hand, generative AI, like the popular language models, is like a human being. It picks up what you're saying, learns from it, and then, using its training data, comes up with something new and helpful in response. That's AI in a nutshell—a computer program that learns from the information they're fed and then uses that learning to make decisions or predictions about new information it encounters.

To understand how AI learns, let's turn to Netflix and spam filters as examples. Netflix's recommendation engine starts with a basic understanding of movies you've liked in the past. However, as you watch more, it learns and adapts to recommend more personalized options in a way that feels intuitive.

Spam filters work on a similar principle. At first, they only have a basic idea of what spam looks like (the unsolicited offers, the too-good-to-be-true promises). But as spammers get craftier, the AI adapts, learning from the patterns of what you mark as spam to become a more effective inbox defender.

Therefore, artificial intelligence is the science of making machines smart. But not smart in the way humans are, with dreams, creativity, and wisdom honed over the years of personal experience. AI is smart in a very calculated, data-driven way. It looks at the vast amounts of information it has, spots patterns, learns from them and then applies what it's learned to make decisions or predictions.

Let's explore the main features that make AI possible: machine learning (ML), natural language processing (NLP), robotics, and computer vision.

Machine learning is how AI learns from data to make predictions or decisions without being directly programmed for the task. AI programs are exposed to vast amounts of training data, like books, articles, emails, and even social media posts. Once the volume of this data becomes substantial enough, the programs start to recognize patterns and context. When AI can recognize patterns, it becomes ready to process data, including language.

Then comes natural language processing (NLP). This lets machines get chatty, translate languages, power voice assistants, and write readable texts. To achieve this, NLP relies on probabilities. Essentially, it calculates what words have the highest chance of being used as a response to the user's input (or 'prompt'). It is a numerical guessing game, but with sufficient training, it can produce wonderful things. It's this system that has given us AI chatbots like Claude, ChatGPT, and many others.

Robotics brings the physical touch, allowing machines to get around spaces or perform physical tasks. For example, an AI-powered robot might vacuum your floors or assemble cars. However, due to the considerable processing power necessary to power sophisticated AI, physical robots are still generally much simpler and more challenging to design. There's still a way to go before a physical robot can paint and physically write poetry.

Lastly, computer vision gives AI the gift of sight. With this technology, the AI can recognize faces, interpret medical images, and drive cars by 'seeing' the road.

Algorithms and data make all these components work together. Algorithms are a set of instructions for solving problems or performing tasks, while data fuels AI's learning. The digital era has seen a colossal leap in collecting, storing, and processing data, making it easier for AI to grow smarter by the day.

But AI isn't just one big, monolithic entity. It's more like a toolset. Each tool has a specialty, like understanding human language, recognizing faces in photos, or suggesting movie night ideas. And just like any other tool, how it's used is up to the user. The tool itself does not have free will or self-awareness, although sometimes it might respond just as a human would.

So don't worry. Artificial intelligence isn't planning to take over the world soon. Rather than seeing it as an all-powerful synthetic human that can do anything or a scary sci-fi concept, consider it a sophisticated digital helper.

However, if AI isn't truly 'intelligent' quite yet, why does it seem so elusive and, at times, uncanny? AI mimics human intelligence, but instead of having a brain made of neurons, it has code. Imagine a computerized scarecrow that scares away birds and then learns the best ways to keep the crops safe based on the birds' behavior. The scarecrow isn't alive, but it has some clever tricks up its sleeve that make it appear more intelligent and human-like than it truly is.

BRIEF HISTORY: THE RISE OF AI

The idea of artificial intelligence has been around for almost as long as human civilization. While humanity never had the means to achieve anything like it until recently, that didn't stop it from dreaming and imagining the possibilities.

One of the best-known examples is the ancient Greek myth of Talos, a giant bronze automaton created by Hephaestus, the god of blacksmiths and fire. According to the story, Talos was tasked to protect the island of Crete by circling its shores three times a day to keep invaders at bay. In a way, Talos is like a mythological automated security system.

Another interesting Greek story is that of Pygmalion, a sculptor who fell in love with a statue he had carved. Seeing his unyielding obsession with the cold, hard marble, Aphrodite brought the statue to life. It could be described as the original virtual girlfriend.

However, the true development of AI saw its inception in the mid-20th century, a time when computers were room-sized super-calculators. In 1950, Alan Turing, a British mathematician, pondered the question, 'Can machines think?' He devised the Turing Test, a clever chat test to see if a computer could fool a human into thinking it was another human. This was the spark that ignited the AI flame.

The Turing Test sets up a blind communication scenario where a human judge interacts with both a human and a machine, but without knowing which is which. The theoretical conversation would happen through a computer interface, keeping the judge in the dark about who or what is on the other side. If the judge can't reliably tell the machine from the human based on their responses alone, the machine would have human-like intelligence. More specifically, it would at least be human-like in terms of generating convincing human-like responses. This test cleverly sidesteps the need to define intelligence precisely and instead focuses on how humans interpret one another's intelligence.

Fast forward to 1956 to the Dartmouth Conference, where the term 'artificial intelligence' was officially coined. This gathering of brilliant minds was optimistic, to say the least. They believed that a machine as intelligent as a human being was just around the corner. However, it was a bit further down the road than they thought.

In the following decades, AI experienced several ups and downs, known as the 'AI winters.' These were periods when research and hype for AI dipped. Funding dried up as initial optimism waned, and the limitations of AI technology became apparent.

AI research froze over, not once but twice—first in the late 1970s and then again in the late 1980s. As overly optimistic expectations crashed into the hard wall of technical limitations, disappointment among the public and investors followed. But, like any good underdog story, AI wasn't down for the count thanks to breakthroughs in machine learning, an explosion of data, and vastly improved computing power.

The 1990s and early 2000s marked an AI renaissance fueled by two developments: the World Wide Web and an exponential increase in computing power. These decades introduced machine learning—where computers learn from data rather than follow explicitly programmed instructions.

A memorable moment from this period was in 1997 when IBM's Deep Blue defeated world chess champion Garry Kasparov. Why was victory in a game such a monumental point in history? It was a demonstration of AI's potential to challenge and surpass human intelligence in specific, highly logical tasks.

Then, deep learning took off in the 2010s. It turned AI from a promising theory to a part of our daily lives. Deep learning is inspired by the structure of the human brain and lets AI perform complex tasks, like recognizing speech and images with striking accuracy.

Perhaps the most relatable breakthrough came in 2011 when IBM's Watson impressed the world by beating Jeopardy! against human champions. The machine's victory in a quiz showed AI's ability to understand and process natural language at a level previously thought impossible.

Not to be outdone, Google DeepMind's AlphaGo took the spotlight in 2016 by winning against Lee Sedol, a world champion in Go. Impressively, this game is even more complex than chess, with near-infinite board configurations.

Today, AI is integrated into daily life in both obvious and subtle ways, from personalized movie recommendations on Netflix to predictive text on smartphones.

An example of AI's current capabilities is the development of tools that can create art or compose music, blurring the lines between human and machine creativity. Large language models, like ChatGPT, Claude, and Gemini, can generate rudimentary poetry and prose. Meanwhile, image generators like Dall-E, Midjourney, and Stable Diffusion create pictures in any artistic style with just a brief description from the user. AI text-to-speech tools like ElevenLabs can mimic the human voice and read your eBooks almost as expressively as a human narrator.

AI continues to push the boundaries of what's possible. Autonomous vehicles and AI-assisted medical diagnoses are in the pipeline. These technologies pave the way for a future where AI's impact transcends daily conveniences and starts solving some of humanity's toughest challenges.

TYPES OF AI: FROM NARROW TO GENERAL

Artificial intelligence can be classified in several ways, but the broadest is the distinction between narrow and general artificial intelligence. Narrow AI is a type of artificial intelligence with tremendous capabilities within one trade. However, it wouldn't know how to handle tasks outside its narrow scope. It's the simpler, more easily achievable form of artificial intelligence that has already taken over.

Most generative AI currently out there falls under narrow AI, at least as of 2024. Yet, the lines are sometimes blurred. For example, language models like ChatGPT and Gemini may communicate directly with an image generator to interpret and create pictures. However, text and image generation are still separate tasks. A language model doesn't 'see' an image in a way a human would. This separation is why you might occasionally get odd results when you ask for a specific picture despite the language model claiming it shows exactly what you requested.

Narrow AI dominates the digital world. For instance, AI Chatbots on websites are friendly (and sometimes not-so-friendly) digital assistants helping you track orders or answer questions about a product. They can understand and respond to specific queries but aren't particularly useful for other prompts.

Algorithms on streaming services, content websites, social media, and shopping sites also count as narrow AI. That's because they collect data about user activity and learn from it. Once they have enough information on a user, they can predict what said user might want to see or buy.

Another good example of narrow AI is autonomous vehicles. They use narrow AI to navigate roads, make split-second decisions, and keep passengers safe. While they may have a long way to go before they can replace human drivers, self-driving vehicles know every traffic rule and road layout. Yet, they don't aspire to learn how to fly a plane; instead, they stick strictly to the task at hand.

Let's look at how these examples of narrow AI work. One way AI can interact with you is through decision trees. For example, when you chat with customer service bots, they pass information through decision trees. These decision trees act like flowcharts that guide the conversation according to your responses.

Meanwhile, when Facebook recognizes your face among a sea of photos, it's thanks to convolutional neural networks. These networks are algorithms that function similarly to the human brain's visual cortex.

Tensors, essentially multi-dimensional arrays, are the backbone for these advanced AI models, including those behind autonomous vehicles and facial recognition. When AI must process complex data, like interpreting a road's layout for a self-driving car or distinguishing your face from millions of others, it uses tensors to organize and manipulate information.

On the other end of the AI spectrum lies artificial general intelligence, or AGI—the true final form of artificial intelligence. AGI is still only a theoretical concept, but given the advancements in the early 2020s, it may be closer than ever before. AGI is meant to match or surpass human intelligence across the board. This AI would be equally adept at composing symphonies, solving complex math problems, and inventing new technologies. It's the ultimate dream of AI research: creating machines that can learn and reason about the world as flexibly and creatively as humans do.

Thrilling research is happening in AI labs to bridge the gap between narrow AI and AGI. Scientists, developers, and machines are working on multimodal AI systems that can handle text, images, and sounds, making sense of them all together. The cutting-edge research seeks to bring together the best of both worlds, creating an AI that's a jack-of-all-trades with a knack for creativity and understanding across the board. For example, imagine talking to a chatbot, like any of the large language models, but this time, the bot can see you, hear you, and perhaps recognize a tune you're humming. This bot might have the capability to understand how you're feeling, play a song you'd like to hear, and perhaps draw an inspiring picture to lift your spirits.

Making machines with the talent to master both Beethoven and calculus goes beyond just a remarkable leap in technology. It also calls into question the essence of cognition itself. The task is akin to teaching a computer to ponder, innovate, and perhaps even dream. Beyond the technical hurdles, such as developing algorithms that can generalize across tasks and contexts, lie profound ethical considerations. Is it possible, or even ethical, to mold these potential digital minds to respect human values and rights while lacking their own rights? The prospect of AGI nudges philosophers and developers to ponder the future of work, privacy, and societal roles. Ethics in technology have always been valuable, but with the prospect of AGI, considering ethics becomes more pressing and necessary than ever.

This is the form of AI that many imagine when they hear the words 'artificial intelligence'. It's also potentially the most unsettling one. The idea of machines that are better at human activity than humans may give you pause. However, just as with narrow AI, if AGI ever becomes a reality, it will still be a tool, and it's up to the programmers and users to apply it responsibly and ethically. For now, general AI is more a subject of sci-fi novels and theoretical discussions than reality.

AI VS. TRADITIONAL COMPUTING: A FRIENDLY RIVALRY

Within traditional computing, every program operates according to a set of predefined instructions. Traditional computer software consists of code written in a programming language, which then converts into 1s and 0s—signals that a computer can understand. It then follows these commands to the letter, with no deviations allowed. You won't get very far if you try to use it for something it wasn't programmed to do. It may display an error or do nothing at all, depending on what you try to do with it.

On the other hand, AI is less limited than a regular program. In truth, code and instruction sets still underpin AI. After all, it's still fundamentally a computer program that cannot substantially exceed its training data. However, rather than just following a fixed set of instructions, AI uses algorithms to process data, learn from it, and make decisions or predictions. As mentioned earlier, machine learning allows it to improve its performance gradually without human intervention.

When a human interacts with it, AI can follow and adjust its responses to user input in a logical way, even if the input is something AI has never been exposed to before. For example, traditional writing assistant software may correct your grammar and offer some rephrasing suggestions. An AI-powered writing assistant could analyze your whole story and provide sophisticated feedback on its content, such as what it liked and what might need some work.

AI shines when it tackles tasks that might make traditional computing struggle. For example, AI in language translation apps gets better at understanding nuances and context the more you and others use it. It learns from vast amounts of text data to provide increasingly accurate translations that sound more natural. A traditional program cannot learn independently; instead, it depends on user input for all its potential growth.

Also, consider predictive analytics. AI can sift through mountains of data to forecast future trends, something way beyond the reach of standard software.

The tech that powers AI includes programming languages like Python. It's a language beloved for its simplicity and versatility. While Python is popular for traditional programming, it's more suitable for AI than other programming languages. Along with frameworks like TensorFlow and PyTorch, Python lets developers handle the complexities of learning from data. Meanwhile, programming languages like C++ or Java, while powerful, are a little more rigid and don't adapt or learn on their own quite as well.

AI's prowess is making real-world impacts across various sectors in ways traditional computing hasn't been able to keep up. For example, in healthcare, AI models predict patient outcomes with uncanny accuracy and speed up drug discovery by analyzing vast datasets for potential treatments.

Finance has seen AI detect fraud better than any human and automate trading, turning the tide in the battle against financial crimes and market manipulation. AI can also attempt to predict market trends and stock fluctuations, which spells some interesting developments in future trade.

Meanwhile, in environmental science, AI climate modeling and wildlife conservation offer insights that help scientists make decisions that might change the future of planet Earth. These case studies highlight how AI complements traditional computing, pushing the boundaries of what's possible with technology.

While comparing AI to traditional computing, let's also give some attention to the difference between AI and the human brain. The human brain is the ultimate adaptive system. It can learn, reason, and create in ways AI may still aspire to achieve. Both artificial intelligence and traditional computing strictly rely on data and code, although in different ways. Meanwhile, experiences, emotions, and consciousness power the human mind in a way unreachable to AI.

However, AI excels in processing and analyzing vast amounts of data better than either humans or traditional computer programs ever could. Its speeds and accuracy at particular tasks, like pattern recognition, are extraordinary. It's also less prone to bias and limitations, making it more challenging for humans to identify patterns and make predictions. However, AI lacks the emotional intelligence and ethical reasoning that come naturally to humans, making this match more complementary than competitive.

Similarly, the relationship between AI and traditional computing isn't a rivalry but rather a partnership. Traditional computing provides the structured, rule-based foundation for AI systems to work as they should. Meanwhile, AI is flexible, adaptable, and somewhat 'human-like', which gives it a distinct value proposition.

CHAPTER 2

UNDERSTANDING HOW AI WORKS

To understand how AI works behind the hood, let's break down the nuts and bolts of what makes AI tick: machine learning (ML) and deep learning. These concepts are the core of how computers manage to do things that were once strictly human territory, like telling cats from dogs in photos or deciding if an email is spam.

Machine learning is what lets computers soak up info and get smarter over time without someone having to hold their hand through every step (as would've been the case with traditional programs). After getting enough information by being fed the same idea (such as a picture of a cat) many times over, the computer learns to spot them on its own by means of machine learning. This is why your inbox is (mostly) free of spam and how Netflix seems to know your movie tastes better than your best friend.

Dig a bit deeper, and you'll find three main ways ML accomplishes all this: supervised, unsupervised, and reinforcement learning. The difference is in whether the learning is from structured data with clear answers, putting together information without explicit instructions, or learning by trial and error.

Then there's deep learning. This uses neural networks, mimicking the human brain's setup, so it can chew on more complex problems. If deep learning were a person, it'd be the one who can solve a Rubik's Cube in under a minute—it tackles tasks by breaking them down into bite-sized pieces, from spotting shapes in a photo to translating languages.

Talking about artificial intelligence is hardly possible without talking about 'real' intelligence first. So, here's something to wrap your head around: the human brain is a network of around 86 billion neurons, all communicating through about 100 trillion connections. Deep learning's neural networks are the tech world's homage to this, albeit on a much, much smaller scale. While they might have millions of artificial neurons, they're still playing catch-up to the complexity of gray matter.

MACHINE LEARNING AND DEEP LEARNING

The first step to understanding how exactly artificial intelligence works is to explain what machine learning is in the first place. Machine learning algorithms let computers learn from data without being directly programmed to perform specific tasks. It's akin to teaching a computer to recognize your cat in photos by showing it thousands of cat pictures. After enough time, it learns to pick out whiskers, pointy ears, and furry tails all on its own. ML is the reason your email can tell spam from important messages and why Netflix seems to understand your binge-watching preferences better than you do. It can predict that you're more likely to binge-watch a sci-fi series after you've just finished another one.

As mentioned, there are three types of learning worth mentioning here: supervised, unsupervised, and reinforcement learning. Supervised learning is like a diligent student with a textbook, where the data is labeled with the correct answers. Unsupervised learning, on the other hand, is akin to sorting a pile of rocks based on their inherent characteristics without any predetermined categories as a guide. Finally, reinforcement learning is trial and error, much like training a canine companion with treats (or by withholding treats) until it learns a trick.

To illustrate the power of ML in action, think about Spotify's Discover Weekly feature—a personal AI DJ that seems to understand your musical tastes better than you do yourself. By analyzing your listening habits and the patterns of users with similar preferences, it curates a playlist of fresh recommendations so you never run out of new tunes to explore.

Now, if ML is the chef, then deep learning is the gourmet recipe that's a bit more complex and refined. It uses something called neural networks, which take directly after the human brain's architecture. There's a vast network of neurons (or nodes) in the brain. In deep learning, layers of algorithms simulate these neurons, with each layer capable of learning a part of a task. For example, when it's processing a photo of a dog, one layer might focus on detecting edges and shapes, another on textures, and yet another on recognizing specific features like tails or noses. This is how deep learning can handle incredibly complex tasks, such as translating languages or driving cars autonomously.

In the human brain, those 86 billion neurons and 100 trillion connections or synapses mentioned earlier are the highways of information transfer that let us learn, think, and react. When we learn something new, the strength of these connections changes; this change is scientifically known as synaptic plasticity, which is foundational for memory and learning.

By contrast, deep learning neural networks consist of layers of artificial neurons or nodes. These layers connect to each other by means of 'weights' that, like synapses, adjust as the network learns from data. However, a decisive difference is in the scale and complexity: while a large deep learning model might boast millions of artificial neurons and billions of connections, it still pales in comparison to the sheer complexity of the human brain. Furthermore, deep learning models learn through exposure to vast datasets. Through them, they adjust their weights via algorithms like backpropagation, which is conceptually different from how learning and creating memories happens in biological neural networks.

The analogy of creating a cartoon version of a city's map to describe deep learning's relation to the brain is fitting. This playful and simplified representation is similar to how deep learning relates to the intricate workings of the human brain.

Just as the cartoon map highlights landmarks and routes while glossing over the minutiae, deep learning extracts and distills the fundamental principles of neural processing and pattern recognition.

It doesn't attempt to replicate the complexity of biological neural networks or their many functions down to the last synapse. Instead, it zeroes in on the core mechanisms that underpin information processing and learning.

Deep learning has been the force behind spectacular advancements across numerous fields, like image and speech recognition, natural language processing, and self-driving vehicles. It can learn from and interpret intricate datasets, and the impressiveness of this ability is undeniable. However, this simplification comes at a cost—a lack of nuanced understanding and general intelligence that define the human brain.

Here's an example that shows this well: while deep learning models can recognize objects in images or translate text with impressive accuracy, they tend to falter with tasks that require common sense, creativity, or emotional intelligence. It's like they can see the individual puzzle pieces but struggle to comprehend the bigger picture.

Yet, there are times when deep learning has achieved remarkable feats. Take AlphaFold, developed by Google's DeepMind, which made a groundbreaking discovery in the field of biology by accurately predicting the 3D shapes of proteins. Imagine trying to solve a complex 3D puzzle, with each piece intricately connected to the next, and you'll have a glimpse of the challenge AlphaFold conquered. This breakthrough holds the secret to unlocking a deeper understanding of diseases and paving the way for the development of new medicines.

Here's another fun fact to chew on: the first neural network in computing was created all the way back in the 1950s, but it took about 60 years to gather enough computational power and data to truly unlock the potential of deep learning. Nowadays, these technologies go far beyond recognizing cats or recommending movies. As we've seen with AlphaFold, they became advanced enough to substantially impact fields like healthcare by predicting diseases from medical images and environmental science by monitoring climate changes at a scale and speed impossible for human researchers.

The secret ingredient making both ML and deep learning possible is data. And not just a sprinkle of data, but heaps and heaps of it. The more data these systems can learn from, the better they get at their tasks. But how do they get all this data? The answer is mainly through data-scraping the Internet and other sources. Think about just how much data flows through the web at all times, and you'll get an idea of what AI can work with. Every minute, users watch 4.7 million videos on YouTube, send 500,000 tweets, and post 49,000 photos on Instagram. All this data feeds into AI systems, teaching them about human preferences, language nuances, and social trends.

Imagine the AI's process of learning from this data as a vast network of water pipes (neurons) with adjustable valves (weights). Water (data) flows through this network, and the system learns the best settings for the valves to direct water to the right destination, much like how neural networks adjust their weights to get the correct output.

This is far from the end of the road for machine learning and deep learning technologies. While they have produced some exceptional results, AI always needs more and more data to stay current and be more accurate. So, researchers are exploring quantum computing to take AI's capabilities even further. Quantum computers use the principles of quantum mechanics to process information in ways traditional computers can't, potentially making AI unimaginably faster and more powerful.

Also, it's less likely to hallucinate, which is when AI "makes something up." It doesn't have a correct answer, but its coding forces it to respond, or when the way it weighs its knowledge leads it to assume incorrect information to be true. However, quantum computing itself is somewhat elusive and theoretical at this point, so both it and AI have a long way to go, likely together.

The human brain is endlessly fascinating, spurring researchers to explore new frontiers in artificial intelligence. The latest neuroscientific discoveries have encouraged researchers to develop models and algorithms that could bridge the gap between machine and biological intelligence.

One exciting avenue they're trying out is neuromorphic computing, which tries to mimic the brain's architecture more closely in hardware. Emulating the way neurons and synapses operate could let these systems potentially process information with the same energy-efficient elegance as our gray matter.

Another idea integrates principles of synaptic plasticity—the ability of brain connections to strengthen or weaken over time—into artificial neural networks. Just as human brains continuously rewire themselves through experience, these plastic networks can dynamically remap their circuitry as they encounter new data.

DATA AND AI

We've already touched upon data with regard to machine learning and deep learning, so let's expand upon the concept of data and AI a bit further. With every click, swipe, and type, you make drops of breadcrumbs along your path that can lead algorithms and AI toward understanding you and, by extension, humanity in general. AI scraping tools collect these breadcrumbs in massive quantities—a concept called 'big data'. Every time you interact with smart devices, use social media or just browse the Internet, you're contributing to a vast ocean of data. For example, Facebook processes about 4 petabytes of data per day, equivalent to a whopping 1 million gigabytes. That's a lot of selfies, status updates, and cat videos fueling their AI to personalize your feed, and then go a step beyond that and learn how humans think and feel.

But raw data is like crude oil. It needs refining. This is where the art of data processing steps in. It turns the raw, messy, and unstructured data into a clean, organized form that AI can understand. Think of it as sorting and labeling every piece of a gigantic Lego set so that you can build something amazing without hunting for the right piece for hours. However, for AI, the structure is instead distilled into numbers that 'weigh' how well each piece of data fits together to create something cohesive. Back to the Lego analogy—the data chunks are the pile of blocks that don't look like any specific object, just blocks. You have to put them together in the right way to create the car, rocket, building, or whatever else the set is supposed to represent.

What that means is that the AI doesn't hold all this data in some giant database that it can pull from at any moment. Instead, the numbers serve as a blueprint for how to arrange words, pieces of imagery, or whatever else the AI needs to process in a way that makes sense.

So, this processed data feeds AI models, teaching them to recognize patterns and make predictions. For example, by showing AI thousands of pictures of dogs and cats, it learns to tell them apart. At first, when the model is new and hasn't learned from enough data, it might confuse these two animal species (and others, like bunnies) and produce something that doesn't look like any specific animal. In fact, the earliest AI image generators would create 'blobs' or random image fractions that made little sense together. Soon enough, they were able to replicate real-world objects and creatures with astonishing accuracy and even make up something entirely unique if the user prompted it. Google's AI, for one, can differentiate between a trillion images, making it the ultimate game of 'I Spy.'

Here's a mind-blowing fact: an AI model called GPT-3, developed by OpenAI, was trained on a dataset estimated to contain about 45 terabytes of text data—that's roughly 45,000 gigabytes or the equivalent of reading about 20 million books!

Internet of Things (IoT) devices, the smart, Internet-connected modern conveniences from smart fridges to fitness trackers, are expected to generate over 73 zettabytes of data by 2025. This tsunami of data from everyday objects provides AI systems with detailed insights into human behavior and environmental conditions, allowing for innovations like predictive maintenance in manufacturing or personalized health recommendations.

While it's clear that AI needs a lot of data to understand the world (and do its tasks), there's something else that deserves attention. The quality of data is as significant as its quantity. An AI trained on biased or inaccurate data will make flawed decisions. For instance, a facial recognition system trained predominantly on one demographic group may struggle to accurately recognize individuals outside that group. This issue could lead to issues of fairness and inclusivity.

The issue of the type of data an AI is trained on brings out the ethical implications of data used in AI. The misuse of personal data for political targeting underscores the importance of ethical data collection processing and the need for regulations. That's why initiatives like GDPR (General Data Protection Regulation) exist—to protect people's privacy while still letting AI learn from as curated and diverse data as possible.

Now, let's take a few moments to appreciate the type of data that AI learns from. AI models trained on decades of weather data offer meteorologists more accurate and timely predictions. That way, the population can be better prepared for disasters, farmers can plan ahead more easily, and it might even optimize renewable energy production.

Tools like Google Translate harness the power of vast text data to bridge the gap between languages. Like a skilled interpreter, it learns from a myriad of sources—books, websites, documents—continuously refining its accuracy and fluency, enabling communication to flow freely across the globe.

It's worth noting that a significant portion of the world's information exists in an unstructured form—text, images, and more. Therefore, natural language processing technologies empower AI to comprehend and process human language from this wealth of unstructured data by turning it into actionable insights. It becomes able to gauge the pulse of public sentiment on a wide range of topics, from brand perception to political views, simply by analyzing social media posts with sentiment analysis algorithms.

The demand for high-quality training data continues to outpace supply. So, AI researchers are exploring new frontiers – such as synthetic data generation. It's a clever approach that involves creating artificial data that is so realistic it can effectively train AI models, opening up new avenues for AI development without compromising privacy or waiting for massive real-world datasets to accumulate. In a way, it means the future seems to hold AI models training other AI models.

ALGORITHMS THAT LEARN

Now that you know how AI learns and what it learns from, let's cast a glance at the instructions that make it learn. Essentially, learning algorithms start as blank slates or, more accurately, like newborns eager to learn about the world. Just as a baby learns to recognize patterns (like distinguishing between day and night), algorithms learn by identifying patterns in the aforementioned data. They do this through a process called training. Training is where AI systems are exposed to vast volumes of data. Each piece of data helps the algorithm make tiny adjustments to its internal settings, which are kind of like tuning a guitar until it sounds just right.

Here's where it gets more interesting—these algorithms aren't just one-hit wonders. They refine their skills as they go. The more data they're exposed to, the better they get at their tasks. For example, a spam filter starts with a basic understanding of what spam looks like. Over time, as it sees more examples, it becomes an expert at catching spam, much like how you get better at spotting unwanted snail mail in the physical mailbox.

Now, armed with all this learned knowledge, AI systems make decisions in many different contexts. Let's say you're using an AI-powered navigation app. The AI algorithm behind it decides the best route using what it's learned about traffic patterns, road closures, and your driving preferences. The app is a smart co-pilot that memorizes every map and traffic report.

Netflix uses learning algorithms to recommend movies and shows. It analyzes billions of records to understand your viewing preferences, making it a personal movie concierge. It's why every recommendation might feel almost eerily relatable.

The success of Google's AlphaGo was due to learning algorithms that improved by playing millions of games against itself, a kind of digital self-reflection. This capacity is something even the most prolific player cannot quite match.

Learning algorithms have cracked languages, too, and humanity's vast network of cultural codes. They can translate between languages with increasing accuracy, learn to generate human-like text, and even create poetry (though we might want to leave the latter to the real poets for now). The most significant difference between traditional, old-school translators and AI-powered ones is that AI-powered translation can comprehend and preserve nuance and context, while traditional tools translate literally and without any broader understanding.

The modern iteration of Google Translate breaks down language barriers daily. This service uses a form of AI called neural machine translation (NMT) to understand and translate languages. Unlike older methods that are translated piece by piece, NMT looks at whole sentences, preserving context and nuance like a polyglot whispering translations in your ear. It allows for real-time conversations between speakers of different languages. The system learns from an enormous corpus of text to endlessly refine its translations.

Initially, AI pioneers had to teach a computer to differentiate between a cat and a croissant using algorithms that learn (yes, it's been a real challenge). That's how image recognition was born. Google Photos is an app that organizes your pictures using this tech. It finds every photo of your cat amidst thousands with just a search. How? Through AI learning from millions of images, recognizing patterns (like the tell-tale whiskers and furry coats) to tell your feline friend apart from breakfast pastries. It's a blend of convolutional neural networks (CNNs) at work, a type of deep learning algorithm specialized in parsing visuals, trained on vast datasets to achieve incredible levels of deduction in the visual department.

Moving from the digital to the wild, AI's algorithms that learn are helping save endangered species. Researchers use AI-powered cameras to snap pictures in the wilderness of animals that are too elusive for humans to spot. AI then sifts through these photos, identifies species, counts individuals, and tracks their movements over time. This data gives conservationists invaluable insights into animal behaviors and population trends without disturbing their natural habitats.

These examples show just how versatile and adaptable AI is and the profound impact of its learning capabilities on daily lives and the world at large.

DEBUNKING MYTHS

While AI has been largely met with excitement and anticipation, it's also drawn some negative attention toward itself. It's no surprise, considering all the dystopian sci-fi that popular culture has exposed us all over the decades. Some of the concerns are understandable and grounded in reality. Many of the worries are a point of discussion among researchers and philosophers interested in the field of AI ethics. However, some of them are also based more on myths than reality. On the other hand, some AI myths may be overly optimistic or have unrealistic expectations of the technology and its current state of development.

The most pressing issue, which is also somewhat of a myth, is the idea that AI will replace the need for human labor. While it's true AI can automate or at least speed up many tasks, its role is more augmentation than replacement. AI can be the ultimate assistant that handles repetitive tasks so you can focus on creative and strategic work. Furthermore, for every job AI transforms or perhaps threatens, it also creates new opportunities in sectors like AI maintenance, programming, and ethical oversight. It's not necessarily a job terminator but a career transformer.

Another misconception is the idea that AI, such as language models like ChatGPT, is 'intelligent' just as humans are. AI excels in specific tasks, like crunching large amounts of data or playing chess, but it lacks general intelligence, emotional understanding, and creativity. If you ask AI to write a poem, it might stitch together something syntactically correct, but, often, it lacks the soul a human touch brings. Or it might do a decent job by accident but may not be able to repeat it time after time. AI is like a highly skilled artist who can only paint by numbers—impressive, but not quite Picasso. That is unless you guide it with careful, thoughtful prompting. That's where the power of human touch becomes the deciding factor.

It's also worth being aware that AI is only as unbiased as the data it's fed. If the data has bias, the AI will also act like a mirror reflecting society's imperfections, human error, or limited scope. That's why AI development employs diverse teams and ethical guidelines.

Remember, AI isn't coming up with ideas on its own. Rather, it's learning from what humans show it, like a child learning from the world around them and the people who influence them.

It may also, at times, seem like AI is 'aware' or has feelings. In fact, there are situations, for example in creative writing, where AI might do better with emotion: AI may be able to portray emotion in a technically accurate way better than some humans. But while AI can recognize patterns in speech or facial expressions that correlate with emotions, it doesn't actually 'feel' anything. When Siri responds to your jokes, it's not genuinely amused. It's programmed to recognize cues and respond appropriately. AI in emotional analysis is more like a thoughtful observer, not an emotional participant.

Onto the next misconception. Considering how fast AI development has been in the early 2020s, it's understandable to anticipate general AI as being just around the corner. But achieving artificial general intelligence is still a distant goal. Experts in the field have vastly different predictions about if and when AGI might become a reality. The predictions range from decades to potentially never. Indeed, we aren't quite sure if it's even possible yet, at least in the form you might imagine it. Researchers are making strides, but the finish line to true AGI is not just around the corner.

Don't think that AI is always good at making decisions or is to be trusted unconditionally. The truth is that AI's decisions are only as good as the data and programming behind them. Picture trying to make a gourmet meal with only fast-food ingredients; the outcome is held back by what you have at the start. Similarly, AI can make errors, especially in complex situations where data may be incomplete or ambiguous. Furthermore, when you prompt it, it's compelled to give an answer even when it might be struggling, so it could decide to hallucinate over refusing to answer. While AI is immensely useful and, for the most part, quite accurate, sometimes its answers should be taken with a pinch of salt.

AI can perform tasks without constant human supervision, but it's not roaming the digital world with free will. Every AI system has boundaries that its creators set up for it. Like a Roomba, a simple, traditional 'robot' roams your house on its own but doesn't decide to clean your neighbor's place on a whim. AI operates within a sandbox, making 'independent' decisions only within a predefined scope.

The term artificial intelligence might evoke visions of sentient robots. After all, human society has created tales of such constructs before any real robots. But in reality, AI encompasses a broad spectrum of capabilities, many of which are quite specific and not 'intelligent' in the way human or even animal intelligence may manifest. For example, an algorithm that predicts stock prices is savvy in finance but won't help you bake a cake. AI's intelligence is special, not universal, at least for now.

Chatbots and virtual assistants have come a long way. Yet, they still can't fully replicate the nuances of human interaction. Have you ever had a conversation with Siri or Alexa that took a hilariously wrong turn? Or even with the more nuanced LLM chatbots like ChatGPT or Claude? While they may understand you better than a virtual assistant, every so often, they'll say something that doesn't work or make it painfully obvious that, despite the clever language or intricate understanding, it's still not a conversation with a person. That's because AI struggles with context, irony, and emotional subtleties. It's getting better at these, but it still has a long way to go. It's like trying to explain why a joke is funny; if you have to explain it, the magic is lost.

Learning for AI can be as bumpy as learning a new skill for humans. Just as you might stumble through your first dance class, AI algorithms often go through a trial-and-error process called training, where mistakes are a necessary part of learning. Sometimes, these mistakes can lead to unexpected or humorous outcomes. The path to AI wisdom is paved with digital faceplants.

CHAPTER 3

ARTIFICIAL INTELLIGENCE IN DAILY LIFE: RECOGNIZING ITS PRESENCE

Tucked in your pocket or maybe now in your hand, smartphones are the Swiss Army Knives of the digital era. They're a gateway to an ever-growing realm of artificial intelligence that makes everyday tasks a bit more like the sci-fi futures many have dreamt about for decades.

In these mini-computers, AI appears in ways that are both outright obvious and more behind-the-scenes. For example, have you ever stopped to wonder how your phone's camera turns average shots into social media-worthy posts? Or how virtual assistants seem to respond to your commands with a level of sass or sophistication? It's all thanks to clever AI algorithms working overtime to predict what you might want, sometimes even before you know it yourself.

As for those moments when you're staring at your screen, wondering what to watch next or which rabbit hole of information to tumble down, AI is the one nudging you toward your next move online, whether obviously or subtly. It learns from your taps, types, and swipes.

So, it's worth taking a closer look at how these technological marvels are quietly (and not so quietly) shaping your life and turning the future into the present.

SMARTPHONES AND AI

It's hardly a surprise that one of the first places you'll find artificial intelligence will be on smartphones. Think of Siri, Google Assistant, and Alexa. They may not be exactly the same as the generative AI that's the current talk of the town, but they certainly qualify. They can tell you the weather, set reminders, send texts, or crack a joke, all without you having to lift a finger. But how can they do this? It's through advanced AI algorithms that they understand natural language, which makes them not too unlike the large language models. These assistants process your voice commands, decipher the context, and respond accordingly. They're always there to help, powered by over 100 billion parameters in some cases, allowing them to understand and generate human-like text.

A part of the smartphone that you might not expect to harness the power of AI is the camera. If your smartphone is recent enough, its camera is smarter than it gets credit for. Beyond capturing pixels, it uses AI to make you look like a photography pro. For that, AI algorithms analyze each frame in real-time, then adjust focus exposure, and can often recognize faces to make everyone look their best (though that might not always be the user's intention). Night mode is AI merging multiple shots at different exposures to create a perfect low-light masterpiece. Portrait mode, blurring the background while keeping your subject sharp, is all thanks to AI understanding depth and focus, mimicking professional DSLR cameras. In 2021, about 1.4 trillion photos were taken, many with smartphones, using AI.

Some broader applications of AI transfer seamlessly right back to the smartphone. Think about a time when you might've been abroad and found yourself playing charades to ask for directions. If that has ever happened to you, you'll be happy to know that those days are fading thanks to AI translation apps that interpret live speech and text in real time across multiple languages. Google's Translatotron, for one, can translate your speech directly into another language, like a pocket interpreter, maintaining your voice tone and cadence.

Your smartphone (or your smartwatch) can keep an eye on your health, too, thanks to AI. Apps can track your steps, monitor your sleep patterns, follow your BMI patterns, analyze your food intake, and more. These health features have been around for several years, but AI has brought them to a whole new level. Advanced health apps use AI to scan for irregular heartbeats or measure stress levels so they can gather insights that were once only possible in a doctor's office. While a pulse oximeter is no longer a common feature on phones, health-centric smart watches may still come with this sensor and others, which collect data about your body and health that specialized personal trainer and health adviser AI can analyze for insights and suggestions. Of course, these tools, even with AI advancements, still aren't a replacement for a professional assessment, but they can be your guide and help you tell when it's a good time to see a doctor.

AI-powered battery management studies how you use the phone—from binge-watching your favorite series to endless scrolling on social media—and then tweaks its energy consumption accordingly. So, your phone now knows the best times to conserve or splurge on power, making sure it lasts as long as you need it to.

AI is also present in security features. Facial recognition locks out intruders by knowing your face better than you do. Meanwhile, anomaly detection finds and reports on unusual activity that doesn't fit your normal phone use. If someone tries to snoop or a mysterious app starts acting up, AI blocks unauthorized access before you even notice.

Also, AI voice-to-text features turn spoken words into text with an impressive accuracy that would make even the most skeptical user nod in approval. AI fine-tunes its proverbial ears to your voice, making miscommunications a thing of the past. Now, your words flow onto the screen as smoothly as they come out of your mouth, all thanks to AI's ever-improving brain.

SOCIAL MEDIA

If there's one place where you might've been feeling the effects of AI firsthand for a while, it's on social media. How does social media AI know you so well? Every like, share, comment, or eye linger on a post is a clue you drop about what tickles your fancy. AI then picks up on these hints. It uses algorithms to analyze your behavior and gradually learn your likes and dislikes. For example, if you enjoy cat videos, you'll see more of them recommended over time. But if you ignore cooking videos, they'll be less likely to show up. However, this is only a small part of the equation. While basic reinforcement has been around for a long time, algorithms have become much more sophisticated. They can now use many aspects of your personality, such as your likes, dislikes, the demographics you belong to, who you interact with, and even what your beliefs are, to recommend posts that seem to fit you just right, even if you never interacted with similar content before. For example, Facebook's news feed algorithm considers thousands of factors, including how often you interact with a friend, page types, and the popularity of a post.

AI sifts through millions of posts, videos, and stories to then push to the forefront those it predicts you'll enjoy the most. Platforms like Instagram and Twitter use these sophisticated AI algorithms to fill your feed with content that's relevant and engaging, or at least what it would assume you would enjoy (after all, even AI can make mistakes now and then). Of course, there's more to it. The algorithm also exists to deduct what products and services you're more likely to purchase or engage with, making AI highly beneficial for advertisers. The idea is to make social media scrolling highly addictive, for better or worse, depending on circumstances and your habits.

AI-powered social media personalization goes beyond the content the news feed recommends. You may have noticed how social media platforms suggest friends you may know or groups you might like. The AI is playing matchmaker here by connecting the dots between your current network and potential new friends or interests. By analyzing shared connections, interests, and activities, it recommends connections that feel surprisingly on point, expanding your social universe one suggestion at a time.

What makes AI in social media particularly remarkable, or perhaps a little eerie, is the ability to handle the vast scale of data collected from billions of users and their interactions. For context, platforms like YouTube process over 500 hours of video uploaded every minute, using AI to recommend the most relevant videos to each user. This takes constant tweaking and updating of algorithms and the data collection approach to keep up with changing user preferences and content trends.

Artificial intelligence is constantly on the lookout, using algorithms to spot and wave off inappropriate, harmful, illegal, or content. AI-driven content moderation keeps social media positive and online communities safe against the riptides of misinformation, bullying, and other online hazards.

AI's sentiment analysis skill reveals the emotional undertones of public opinion. They sift through tweets, posts, and comments to pick up on patterns of joy, frustration, and everything in between. It paints a broad-strokes picture of how the world feels about hot topics and trends. Companies and creators get a sneak peek into what makes their audience tick. AI can interpret the subtle nuances of language to serve up insights that are as informative as they are fascinating.

Visuals turn into words with automatic caption generation and image recognition. These features make the Internet more accessible for people with disabilities and searchable in general. When scrolling through a sea of images, AI tells you what's in each picture and crafts neat, concise captions on the fly. This tech is particularly desirable for those who rely on screen readers to explore the World Wide Web. It enhances searchability, too, so you can find a needle-in-a-digital-haystack image with just a few keystrokes.

ONLINE SHOPPING

Take a moment to pay attention to the 'You might also like' section. Here, AI is working as a behind-the-scenes shopping analyst who wants to sell you items relevant to your past purchases, interests, things you check out, and perhaps things you never thought you needed until you saw it. It remembers practically every item you've ever glanced at, then suggests similar goodies you're likely to enjoy. It even compares you to other shoppers who might have similar tastes and recommends things they usually buy. This is powered by recommendation systems, a sophisticated AI technology that analyzes your browsing and buying history, compares it with millions of other users to find patterns and preferences, and then curates a list. So, when you see a suggestion for a funky teapot right after you've been eyeing some tea sets, it's AI making those connections.

AI is ingrained into online shopping in many other ways, too. The emails you receive and the deals that pop up on your screen are all infused with AI. Not only that, but algorithms also analyze your broader internet usage and use this data to recommend products based on your searches, videos you watch, places you visit, and, some say, even your conversations. However, the last one might be taken with a grain of salt. This personalization magic is possible thanks to machine learning algorithms that constantly learn from your interactions, refining their understanding of your tastes over time. If you're a pet lover, you might find your homepage showing pet care products, pet food deals, or the latest in pet tech if you've recently browsed pet pictures on Instagram.

Online fashion shopping comes with an extra set of challenges compared to shopping for household items and similar, like finding the size that fits. In AI's virtual fitting rooms, algorithms predict the right fit using your measurements and past purchases, which cuts down on the guesswork and the hassle of returns. It may not be a perfect replacement for physically being there and trying the garment on (or visiting a tailor), but it is a substantial step forward.

AI also helps by sifting through thousands of product reviews to highlight the information most relevant to you, summarizing sentiments, and pointing out common praises or complaints. This way, you get the scoop without having to dig through a mountain of feedback. It might not work for everyone, but it makes reading reviews so much quicker, so you can get on with the shopping.

On the flip side, AI helps retailers manage their inventory more effectively by predicting trends, demand, and optimal strategies for setting prices that are neither too high nor too low. This means you're more likely to find what you want in stock and at the best price, thanks to AI's behind-the-scenes number crunching.

AR, or augmented reality, makes it easy to try on glasses or test makeup shades without setting foot in a store. Let's say you're considering a slick pair of sunglasses online. Using AI, augmented reality lets you see them on your face, turning your phone into a virtual mirror. Makeup apps take it further, allowing you to play with eyeshadow colors, lipsticks, or foundation shades, seeing exactly how they look on you in real time.

AI IN HOME DEVICES

Artificial intelligence is closer to home than you might think, literally speaking. The Internet of Things (IoT) and smart homes are concepts that have been around for several years now. These employ the idea of a technologically interconnected home where you can control most of your devices from a single spot (such as your smartphone) and adjust everything with a few clicks or taps. Alternatively, the IoT system could be connected to a control device through which you communicate with a virtual assistant, such as Alexa or Echo. IoT itself is already futuristic enough, but now advanced artificial intelligence is taking it even further. Every single one of these devices is on the path of becoming even more integrated and 'smarter than smart'.

For one, AI saves you the trouble of fiddling with your thermostat. Smart thermostats like Nest or Ecobee learn your schedule and temperature preferences to keep every room in the house just right, no matter the season. They can sense when you're away and adjust the temperature to save energy (and money).

AI-powered energy management systems make homes run like well-oiled machines with undisturbed performance but considerable optimization. These systems smartly decide when to dial down the energy use of certain appliances and when to ramp it up, so everything runs as it's supposed to without wasting a watt. Examples could be your washing machine knowing the best time to run based on electricity rates or your heating system adjusting itself based on the weather forecast. The power management system is constantly looking for ways to save money on your energy bill without you having to lift a finger or sacrifice comfort. These smart-systems learn your habits and preferences over time. They mean no more shocking energy bills, just a cozy, cost-effective home that takes care of itself and the planet.

Smart lights, such as Philips Hue, might not be smart at advanced AI levels, but they are still worth mentioning. They can make your living space look completely different with the tap of an app or a voice command. If you want to relax, you can set a sunset scene. But when you decide to host a party, cue the disco lights. These lights can also mimic natural sunlight to help you wake up gently in the morning. But how would AI improve the lights of all things? Believe it or not, light, and more specifically, color accuracy, temperature, and intensity, have a much more substantial impact on human mood and health than you might imagine. It's fair to imagine AI-controlled smart home systems that adjust lights automatically to improve visibility around the house for different tasks, your mood, sleep schedule, and so forth.

The 'primitive AI' voice assistants like Amazon's Alexa, Google Assistant, and Apple's Siri, the voices of many homes, will improve through generative AI and machine learning. They control devices, play music, set reminders, and even order pizza, all with just your voice. Now, picture these same assistants but with the understanding and nuance of your favorite chatbots, such as Copilot or Gemini. Developments are already in progress.

Smart security cameras and systems like Ring or Arlo keep an eye on your home. They send alerts to your phone if something seems to be amiss. They can distinguish between a delivery person and an unwelcome visitor, offering peace of mind whether you're at home or away. Security of this kind is one of the best places to employ AI, thanks to its ability to learn on its own from patterns and user input. It could even keep track of ongoing threats in the area.

Robotic vacuums like the Roomba have already been that little sprinkle of 'futurism' that entered homes decades ago, but they're getting smart home and AI upgrades, too. They will still roam your home, sucking up dust and debris, but can do it better now. Sensors and AI let them learn the layout of your house so they can now dodge obstacles and focus on higher-traffic areas. Eventually, cameras, AI, and intelligent navigation may even let them overcome their greatest adversary: stairs.

Artificial intelligence could also allow your fridge to keep track of your groceries, suggest recipes based on what you have, and order food and ingredients when low. Smart fridges like Samsung's Family Hub make this a reality, turning your kitchen into a command center for meal planning and more. It saves so much time and energy that you might otherwise spend doing food prep and grocery shopping, two potentially daunting but undeniably essential tasks.

There are other kitchen appliances that could help you cook like a gourmet chef beyond just the strikingly smart fridge. For example, the June Oven uses AI and machine learning to recognize the food you put inside and automatically suggest the best way to cook it to perfection. This allows you to roast chicken or bake cookies like a professional cook, or reheat pizza into crispy goodness without burning it ever again.

Imagine having a personal chef whispering culinary secrets and guidance in your ear, except it's not a chef—it's your smart device using generative AI. These AI-powered cooking assistants make kitchen novices into seasoned chefs (almost) with step-by-step guidance in a range of tasks, from dicing onions to mastering the art of French sauces. Smart kitchen devices act like a cookbook that talks back, answering your questions and offering substitutions when you realize you're out of an ingredient. Furthermore, they learn from your preferences to share suggestions about meals based on your taste, dietary restrictions, and what's in your fridge.

This technology also makes a washing machine capable of telling apart silk, denim, or your gym socks. The smart washing machine is a marvel of AI that can detect the fabric type of your clothes and tweak the washing settings to match. The device helps you avoid the ever-questionable guesswork that can lead to you accidentally shrinking your favorite sweater. These clever machines assess the load, pick the perfect temperature, spin speed, and cycle, so your clothes come out spotless and well cared for every time. They can even advise on the necessary amount of detergent, making laundry day a breeze.

For those who love the idea of homegrown herbs but lack the gardening know-how or forget to water their plants, smart gardens like the Click & Grow Smart Garden can come to the rescue. These compact indoor gardens use AI to ensure your plants receive the optimal amount of light, water, and nutrients, turning anyone into a green thumb. It's like having a tiny, automated farm on your kitchen counter.

Pet owners can now rely on smart pet feeders like the Petnet SmartFeeder to keep their furry friends fed on a regular schedule, even when they're not home. And yet again, AI makes it better. It lets these devices adjust the portion size depending on the pet's age, weight, activity, and preference. They can also send you notifications when it's time to refill the food supply or get more food.

AI-enhanced sleep aids like the Dodow are amazing for those struggling to get a good night's sleep, which seems to be a common woe of modern life. They project a soft, rhythmic light onto the ceiling to slow down your breathing and help you drift off to sleep more naturally. Then, other connected devices monitor your sleep patterns and adjust the environment to improve your sleep quality by adjusting the room temperature or playing soothing sounds. All this is science-based and adjustable, with machine learning powering its clever behavior.

There are even smart mirrors now. Clearly, they aren't just for checking your reflection or putting on makeup but act as a digital personal stylist and beautician. They analyze your outfit, give fashion and cosmetics tips, and simulate how different clothes would look on you without having to try them on. Some offer more detailed beauty advice with skin analysis or let you virtually try on makeup.

AI AND ASSISTIVE TECHNOLOGY

One of the somewhat overlooked but immensely significant applications of artificial intelligence is in the field of assistive technology for people with disabilities. Picture a digital world that's not just smart but also open to everyone, including people with disabilities. These technologies harness what's already available to create accessible gadgets and features. That's the promise AI brings to digital accessibility. It takes the online experience from 'one-size-fits-all' to 'tailored to fit you', so everyone gets to participate, engage, and benefit from the digital revolution, regardless of their abilities.

For starters, AI has a considerable and growing impact on how visually impaired people interact with the digital universe. Screen readers are getting a major AI upgrade. AI technologies now go beyond just reading text on a screen and can describe images, analyze and interpret complex visuals, and guide users through websites. A visually impaired person can now browse a photo-heavy site and get accurate, descriptive narration of each picture. This is an example of AI making the web more inclusive, one image at a time.

Then there's the magic AI that works similarly for people with hearing impairments. Real-time speech-to-text transcriptions and AI-powered sign language interpreters on video calls are breaking down communication barriers. They are essentially a personal interpreter by your side and can deployed in a number of settings, whether that be in a work meeting or watching a live stream. It's much more consistent and affordable than a professional human interpreter, whose availability is limited. These tools enable easy interaction with media and allow users to connect with others on an equal footing.

While most artificial intelligence appears in software form, it might come as a surprise that AI has also had a positive impact on people with mobility challenges. Voice-controlled smart home devices powered by AI turn spoken commands into action helping in ways such as turning off lights or posting on social media. This 'digital butler' learns and adapts to users' routines and preferences. The benefit is in increased independence and control over everyday tasks and online interactions.

Not to mention, AI helps individuals with learning disabilities by providing personalized learning. It adapts content to match each user's learning style, pace, and expectations, turning the daunting sea of information online into manageable, engaging streams. AI is making learning more accessible and enjoyable by breaking down complex ideas into simpler concepts or offering alternative formats like audio or interactive content.

AI FOR HOME COOKING

Here's something rather fun that you can use AI at home for. If you love to cook, add some AI magic to the cooking routine and watch your meals become like something out of a fancy restaurant. Some forms of AI can seriously up your kitchen game, making cooking less of a chore and more of a fun experiment. Picture this: you're prepping dinner, and your smart oven already knows the perfect settings for your lasagna. No more guessing or Googling—just pop it in, and the oven takes over, adjusting the temperature and cooking time for you. It's like having a mini sous-chef that ensures everything comes out just right every time.

And then there's the recipe dilemma. We've all been there, standing in front of the fridge, staring at random ingredients and thinking, "What on earth can I make with this?" This is where AI-powered recipe apps like Whisk or Tasty come in handy. You just punch in the ingredients you have, and voilà, the app churns out a bunch of recipes tailored to what's in your kitchen. It's perfect for those moments when you have half a bell pepper, a leftover chicken breast, and a random assortment of spices.

AI doesn't just help with recipes and cooking times. It can also assist with the nitty-gritty of measuring ingredients. Enter smart scales. These gadgets do more than weigh your flour. They connect to your smartphone, sync with recipe apps, and guide you through the entire cooking process. Imagine a scale that adjusts ingredient quantities on the fly if you decide to cook for four people instead of two. Some even suggest healthier ingredient swaps, so you can feel a bit better about indulging in that double chocolate cake.

If you enjoy planning meals, apps like Mealime and Yummly use AI to create custom meal plans based on your dietary preferences, nutritional goals, and even your weekly schedule. You can plan out your entire week's meals in just a few minutes. Plus, these apps often generate a shopping list for you, so you know exactly what to buy at the grocery store. It takes the hassle out of figuring out what to cook each day and helps you stick to your health goals without much effort. Imagine AI taking care of the meal planning while you just enjoy the delicious results.

And let's not forget about smart fridges. These aren't just regular fridges with a fancy screen. They're smart, AI-boosted fridges with a fancy screen. They can keep track of what's inside, suggest recipes based on what's about to expire, and even add items to your shopping list. The fridge itself is like a kitchen assistant that makes sure you never run out of milk or let your fruits or veggies go bad.

AI IN PERSONAL SAFETY

Let's talk about how AI can make your life safer, too. Think about those personal alarms that you can take with you. It's the ones you carry around that are supposed to scare off attackers with a loud noise. Now, picture an AI-powered version that doesn't just make a racket but also texts your friends and family if it detects something fishy. It's like having a super-alert buddy who always has your back.

Then there are those fancy wearable devices. Sure, they count steps, but they also keep tabs on your heart rate and oxygen levels. Say you're out for a jog and suddenly feel off—these smart gadgets can ping your emergency contacts if your vitals go wonky. It's like having a health guardian on your wrist, always looking out for you.

Don't forget about the AI apps that track your location. It might sound unsettling to some, but it can be good for safety, especially when your friends or family can know where you are or if you're in trouble. Apps like bSafe, Life360, and Noonlight can be lifesavers, literally. If you're walking home late at night and feel a bit uneasy, they can make you feel better. These apps track your journey in real time, and if you don't check in or veer off your usual route, they can alert your friends or family. Your digital chaperone will you get home safe and let everyone know that you're alright.

AI can clearly respond to emergencies and it may also prevent them. Some smart home systems use AI to get to know your daily routine. If something's out of the ordinary—like a door left open or unusual activity in your backyard—it'll let you know. It's like having a home security system that's always learning and adapting to keep you safe.

AI can even help while you're driving. Some apps monitor your driving habits and alert you if you start to drift or drive erratically. They can also notify emergency contacts if you're involved in an accident, like a co-pilot always paying attention, even when you're not.

In the community, AI-powered apps can analyze local crime data and send alerts if there's an increase in incidents nearby. The AI could be your new neighborhood watchdog, helping everyone stay informed and proactive about their safety.

Lastly, AI helps with emergency preparedness. Smart weather apps can predict severe weather more accurately and provide timely alerts, giving you more time to prepare and stay safe, especially if you live somewhere with extreme weather.

CHAPTER 4

AI AT WORK: IMPROVING PRODUCTIVITY AND CREATIVITY

Let's talk about something everyone strives for but sometimes finds elusive: productivity. In our complex digital world, it's no wonder we look to the same source to find ways to untangle the complexity and streamline our daily grind. AI is the partner in the quest to reclaim time, organize chaos, and boost efficiency. AI can mean that your emails sort themselves, your schedule aligns on its own, and your projects practically manage themselves.

But the impact of AI stretches far beyond making to-do lists more manageable. AI is breaking the mold in creativity, challenging the notion that creativity is solely a human trait. AI tools can compose music, generate art, write stories, and produce videos. AI is becoming a creative co-creator.

It also steps up as a critical decision-making partner. In a world drowning in data, AI's ability to sift through the noise and unearth valuable insights is invaluable in practically every industry imaginable.

PRODUCTIVITY TOOLS

Productivity tools are one of the most obvious and common applications of AI. Google and other email providers use machine learning algorithms to categorize emails into tabs and reminders to make them more curated and relevant. They automatically distinguish between personal messages, subscriptions, and work-related communications. Segmentation is possible thanks to analyzing millions of data points from email patterns. It's how the system prioritizes your inbox without manual input, although you still have the reign to modify or disable this feature if you so desire.

Smart Reply is a feature introduced by Google that can suggest quick responses to emails by understanding the message's content. Emails are some of the most repetitive work-related tasks, so it comes as no surprise that this feature has quickly garnered widespread adoption.

AI is the workhorse in the background of project and task management, too. Asana, for example, incorporates AI to personalize task recommendations, automate routine assignments, break tasks down into bite-sized chunks, cleverly organize the workflow, and predict deadlines with startling accuracy. It does so by analyzing past project data, learning from completion times, and adjusting future timelines accordingly. The system effectively 'learns' your work habits and adapts to them so you can work more efficiently without stepping out of your comfort zone too much.

Scheduling is another perennial time sink that AI is here to tackle and defeat. AI schedulers like x.ai or Google's Calendar can negotiate meeting times on their own across different calendars. They aren't entirely number-fixated either and can also consider individual preferences for meeting times, durations, and formats. This way, more people are likely to attend a meeting if its schedule works for the highest possible number of people. How exactly does AI accomplish this? Sophisticated natural language processing techniques parse emails or chat messages for relevant scheduling information. Then machine learning models are used to adapt to user feedback and improve accuracy over time.

Let's talk about document management now. Managing documents, especially PDFs, can be time-consuming and frustrating. Scanning and manually inputting data from physical documents is tedious, prone to errors and inefficiencies, and, truth be told, rather boring. Searching for specific information within a collection of digital documents can be as daunting as trying to find a needle in a haystack.

Adobe's Sensei uses artificial intelligence to simplify this undoubtedly arduous task of managing PDFs and other documents. Optical character recognition (OCR) and machine learning algorithms combine to automatically extract data from scanned documents, convert them into editable formats, and suggest relevant actions in the content when possible. Sensei and similar tools significantly reduce the need for manual data entry and make documents much more searchable.

There is also AI's impact on money management, both for individuals at home and for businesses big and small. Take Mint for personal budgets or QuickBooks for companies as examples. They use AI to sort transactions, keep an eye on how you generally spend money, protect you from fraud, and give tips about clever budgeting. The tools go through tons of transactions instantly to give you a heads-up on where your money is going and how to save it. For businesses, this kind of AI insight spots trends that could tell if the business is improving its bottom line or potentially risks losing it. They can also advise on potentially lucrative investments. AI makes surprises in the balance sheet less likely, especially the unwanted kind.

Einstein AI, a feature of Salesforce's CRM platform, takes customer relationship management to a new level with data-driven predictions and suggestions. It analyzes past customer interactions and outcomes to forecast sales trends, find promising leads for companies to follow, and recommend the next best action for specific clients. When sales strategies are more personal to each client, a customer is more likely to engage with a service or buy a product, and human strategists wouldn't be able to match the level of personalization AI makes possible.

Einstein AI uses hard data to make informed recommendations by studying patterns in customer behavior and sales outcomes. It takes the guesswork out of sales and provides a more scientific, data-driven methodology. For example, Einstein AI might analyze a client's purchase history, communication records, and demographic data to predict their likelihood of buying a particular product or service. It could then recommend specific talking points, marketing materials, or pricing strategies to make said client more likely to buy or subscribe. It might also identify a high-value lead based on the company's size, industry, and online activity and suggest outreach efforts accordingly.

AI transcription services like Otter.ai use the power of speech recognition and natural language processing to transcribe conversations in real-time. They distinguish between speakers and capture the essence of discussions with striking, almost human accuracy.

These AI assistants also go a step further by highlighting points and generating concise summaries that distill the most crucial information. However, the true value of such technology is in its ability to enhance team collaboration and productivity. No more scrambling to recall details or missing out on important points. With accurate transcripts and summaries at your fingertips, you can easily revisit meetings and share insights. Critical information is never lost in the ether.

Language learning apps using artificial intelligence, such as Duolingo, help you learn a language as you would with a personal human tutor. They analyze your responses to find patterns in your mistakes and adjust subsequent lessons to address areas of difficulty.

Here's how they accomplish this: the apps employ spaced repetition algorithms to determine the optimal timing for reviewing certain concepts so users like you can retain the information over an extended period. The adaptive learning technique mimics the responsiveness of a personal tutor who knows your strengths and weaknesses and modifies the curriculum to accommodate them.

The backbone of these advancements is the vast amount of data AI systems can process, from which they learn and make predictions. For email sorting, AI algorithms train using billions of emails, learning to tell apart spam from important messages based on subtle patterns and user interactions. In task management, AI examines historical project data to forecast timelines and identify potential bottlenecks. Scheduling tools learn from your preferences and adjustments, refining their understanding of your ideal workday layout.

CREATIVE AI

There's a new kind of artist that's entered the scene and made sure art will never be the same again: AI. In fact, creative, generative AI is the form of artificial intelligence that has received the most attention, both positive and critical, and is the main subject in almost any AI discussion. It's reshaping music, art, writing, and more, proving that creativity isn't just a human trait anymore. It hasn't been without criticism, but it should be regarded as a tool rather than a replacement for human creativity. So, let's look at the bright side instead and examine just some of the emerging creative AI tools.

Machines as music composers are now a reality. AI systems like AIVA (Artificial Intelligence Virtual Artist) are composing symphonies, pop songs, indie music, and film scores. AIVA analyzes thousands of pieces of music to understand patterns and structures in compositions and then uses this knowledge to create original pieces. It has already garnered a substantial following. Artists and producers are collaborating with AI to explore new soundscapes, resulting in albums where humans and machines share the credits.

There is also Amper Music, an AI music composition tool for digital content creators. It lets users create unique soundtracks by specifying a few parameters, like mood and style, without needing any musical expertise.

Suno is another example. It's an online AI music generator where you can make songs (or instrumentals) of almost any genre (or, at least, the ones the AI has been exposed to). In a prompt, you can specify the genre, style, mood, theme, singer voice, and more. Furthermore, you can let the tool generate its own lyrics based on your prompt, insert your own lyrics, or generate them using an AI language mode.

Landr is a platform that uses AI for music mastering. It does instant, professional-quality audio mastering. To make this possible, it analyses your track and applies adjustments to polish the sound. If you need a remastered audio in a pinch and can't do it yourself, it's an excellent alternative.

ElevenLabs is a text-to-speech tool that can read and narrate text using high-quality voices that sound nearly indistinguishable from human narrators. It may seem odd at first to group ElevenLabs together with creative AI tools, but it begins to make sense once you realize that this tool is incredibly useful for creating entire audiobooks, potentially even with multiple personas for each character. You can adjust the expressiveness and emotion in voice generation to capture the feelings and 'voice' of your characters just as you imagine them. This makes audiobook production much more accessible for indie publishers who may not have the resources to finance a human-read audiobook. You can even clone your own voice and let AI narrate your book the way you would do it. Other text-to-speech tools, like Google WaveNet and even GPT, are catching up on the success of ElevenLabs.

AI is a digital Picasso of the art world. AI-powered tools can turn sketches into detailed artworks or generate entirely new pieces from scratch with just a prompt. Projects like DeepArt use neural networks to apply the styles of famous painters to any photo, effectively turning your selfie into a Van Gogh masterpiece. Meanwhile, OpenAI's DALL-E can generate images from textual descriptions. No matter what you come up with, from whimsical animals to futuristic cityscapes, it can do it. MidJourney and Stable Diffusion are other examples of this same prompt-based image generation technology. Better yet, these tools are becoming able to spell proper words and sentences in graphic form, something that's been a major struggle for early image generators. This way, they could generate believable posters, book covers, or just images that have some text in them.

While some might think AI art is just a copy or a hodgepodge of existing artwork, some of the more surreal examples of its application prove that AI can indeed dream up visuals that have never been seen before.

Originally developed by Google, DeepDream gives you a peek into how AI interprets and processes images, creating surreal, dream-like pictures by enhancing and over-interpreting the patterns it finds in photos.

Artbreeder is an AI platform that allows users to create images by blending different photos together using generative adversarial networks (GANs). It's particularly popular for character design, landscapes, and abstract art. This matters since image generators that rely strictly on prompts, like Dall-E, still don't do too well with generating consistent, serialized images, like multiple images of the same character or location.

Runway ML is a creative toolkit using AI that can do many things simultaneously, like video editing enhancements or generating synthetic media. It's accessible for creatives without technical backgrounds and is easy to learn how to use.

AI is also leaving a mark in the world of words. AI writing tools are becoming increasingly sophisticated in doing tasks like generating poetry or drafting news articles. OpenAI's GPT can produce essays, jokes, and poetry that some might find indistinguishable from human-written text. However, it's certainly not about replacing novelists or journalists; it's being used to aid writers in overcoming writer's block or generating creative content ideas.

Of course, AI content generation has also been met with some pushback, especially in terms of article generation and creative writing. As a response, many AI content detectors, such as ZeroGPT, Copyleaks, Writer.com, and Originality.ai, have appeared to detect and report on the use of AI in text and publishing. These tools are powered by AI, and their results are based on an AI's ability to detect another AI (or potentially the same model detecting itself). Therefore, it's worth noting that, while useful when you need purely original content, these results are still to be taken with a pinch of salt.

While not a tool you can use directly without some programming knowledge, several applications use GPT-3's (and now GPT-4's) capabilities for creative writing, coding, marketing, and generating business ideas. It can generate almost human-like text based on prompts on any subject. That's why it has been integrated into platforms like Sudowrite, which helps authors brainstorm and overcome writer's block.

Speaking of Sudowrite, this tool for writers has quite a few options that make it appealing and useful in beating writer's block. One of the most useful features is the integration of many language models beyond GPT-3 and 4. The software can generate text or rewrites using almost any popular language model, like Claude, Gemini, Mythomax, Goliath, Mistral, and more. Furthermore, new models are added regularly. Another nifty feature is the inclusion of plugins that can do nearly anything, from developmental editing, story analysis, sensor-rich rephrasing, character discovery, and early drafting to role-playing the characters in your scenes to give insights into their thoughts.

There is also NovelCrafter, a tool with a similar goal but a different approach. Its standout feature is the Codex, which holds detailed and well-organized information about your story, characters, setting, world-building, magic systems, and more. Much like Sudowrite, it can employ many different language models, like GPT, Claude, Goliath, and others, for discussion and writing assistance. Both of these tools also have access to less censored versions of these language models compared to their commercial iterations, like ChatGPT.

ShortlyAI also focuses on writing assistance. It uses powerful AI to help you write stories, articles, or any kind of text. You provide a prompt, and it generates text to continue your story, offering endless possibilities for creativity. And much like the name suggests, it's pretty easy to get into and learn.

AI is stepping onto the film set as well. It's being used to script short films, assist in animating sequences, predict box office success, and numerous other tasks. The short film Sunspring was written by an AI and starred human actors. This film shows how AI can contribute to scriptwriting by offering narratives that, while sometimes nonsensical, spark creativity and new approaches to storytelling. Much like in creative writing, the trick is to acknowledge its limits and use it as a tool to speed up creation and expand or spark creativity.

Purely AI-generated content is still rarely good enough to deeply engage audiences. At the moment, it often relies on cliches, overused tropes, or concepts that may lack nuance. However, it's immensely useful when you want to expand upon an idea and complement your workflow.

Synthesia creates synthetic media, allowing users to generate videos from text. These aren't complex videos, like movies, but they're advanced enough to create virtual presenters who act and talk in a natural and approachable manner. It's particularly useful for creating educational content, presentations, advertisements, or news segments without a physical presenter.

Runway ML, mentioned above, also offers features for video creators, including tools for automating video editing tasks, generating visual effects, or altering video content with AI algorithms.

There's also Sora, an OpenAI project still in the pipeline as of early 2024 but likely to become commercially available later in the year. It's a video generation tool that takes it a step ahead of the likes of Synthesia. Instead of the relatively simple AI mocap, like creating a virtual presenter, Sora simulates real physics using AI. This way, it can create incredibly detailed short videos with believable motion and three-dimensionality.

In video gaming, AI is not just behind the scenes making NPCs (non-player characters) smarter. Indeed, the term AI has been used to describe NPC behavior since almost the dawn of gaming, but now there is a bit of a double meaning. Generative and creative AI can simulate more realistic conversations and branching paths never seen before. AI also helps design game levels and storylines for dynamic gaming that adapt to the player's style. This means games are becoming more immersive and personalized through the next-level procedural generation that far exceeds anything available in the past.

Promethean AI assists game developers by automating the creation of 3D environments. Developers can specify the type of scene they want, and Promethean AI builds it. The tool makes iterations and creativity in game design much more brisk.

AI in fashion is like a futuristic stylist. It predicts trends by analyzing social media and online data and designing clothes through generative adversarial networks (GANs). It can customize user experiences in online shopping and integrate them into smart mirrors that match your style and give you ideas for what to wear and how it might look on you.

While not a tool available for public use, Stitch Fix uses sophisticated AI algorithms to personalize clothing recommendations for its users. It's a great example of how AI can understand personal style and preferences in the fashion industry.

In every virtual brush stroke, note, and pixel, AI's impact on the creative industries is undeniable. Together, algorithms and artistry push the boundaries of what's possible. AI continues to learn from human creativity and is also teaching us to view art and creation through a new lens, one where technology and human imagination combine to explore uncharted territories of expression.

DECISION-MAKING SUPPORT

AI's decision-support role comes to life through its ability to handle 'big data'—the colossal, ever-growing mass of information generated by digital activity, from social media posts to transaction records. Big data is a fascinating and perhaps intimidating phenomenon, given just how much data the world produces each minute and the astonishing implications of this. Traditional data analysis methods can't keep up, but AI, with its machine learning muscles, can not only keep pace but sprint ahead.

AI plunges into this data ocean and surfaces with insights that can predict consumer behavior, identify market trends, foresee potential supply chain disruptions, predict social trends, manage crises, and more. For example, retail giants like Amazon use AI to analyze purchasing patterns to stock products more efficiently and tailor recommendations to individual customers.

In the financial sector, AI analyses market data to make predictions about stock prices or identify fraud patterns before they can cause significant damage. Banks and investment firms leverage AI to crunch numbers at an unprecedented scale, giving clients data-driven investment advice.

In addition to managing inventory, AI also boosts customer satisfaction through personalization. It studies what customers look at and buy to suggest items that align with their tastes and even changes websites to match their browsing style. This personal touch keeps customers coming back for more, leading to increased sales.

Healthcare is another field where AI's decision-support capabilities shine. The 2020 COVID-19 pandemic has put healthcare into the spotlight, and major breakthroughs in AI happened at almost the same time. Unsurprisingly, the two spheres of interest were meant to converge. By analyzing patient data and medical records, AI can help doctors diagnose diseases earlier and with greater accuracy. It's a diagnostic super-assistant that can spot the early signs of conditions such as cancer or heart disease, potentially saving lives through early intervention.

In marketing, AI helps companies understand their audience like never before. Through sentiment analysis of social media and online content, AI can gauge public opinion about products or brands. The insights it gathers help marketing strategies resonate more deeply with target demographics.

Cities around the world are turning to AI to improve traffic flow, reduce energy consumption, cut down on traffic jams, and improve public safety. AI can predict traffic congestion and suggest alternative routes in real-time by analyzing data from sensors, traffic cameras, and GPS signals. It effectively reduces commute times and pollution. Additionally, AI-powered systems monitor utility usage across cities, enabling dynamic pricing and conservation efforts that lead to more sustainable urban environments.

Moving on to agriculture, AI is making waves by analyzing data from satellite images, weather forecasts, and soil sensors to help farmers make better decisions about planting, irrigation, and harvesting. AI systems can predict crop yields and monitor crop health so farmers can know what to expect about the upcoming harvest. It can also identify areas at risk for pests or diseases so workers can act swiftly. These precision farming practices increase efficiency, reduce waste, and eventually result in better and healthier crops.

AI algorithms in human resources have become adept at analyzing resumes, assessing a candidate's qualifications, and predicting how well they might fit within a company. This way, HR representatives can spend less time analyzing every piece of information, making hiring easier and quicker.

However, AI's impact doesn't stop at recruitment. These tools also evaluate employee engagement and productivity to help companies boost workplace satisfaction and reduce turnover rates. Employers can use these insights to create an environment where more people will want to work and remain loyal.

Utility companies use AI to forecast energy demand and distribute electricity more evenly and fairly. Consumption patterns and peak demand periods that AI detects let utility companies manage energy resources better. This helps in reducing operational costs and contributes to integrating renewable energy sources into the grid.

Sports teams and athletes use AI to analyze performance data to improve training regimens and strategies. Data from video footage, wearable sensors, and performance stats allow AI to identify patterns and areas for player and strategy improvement. It can then tell coaches and players what and how to modify their training and gameplay through insights that were previously unattainable.

AI's decision-support prowess also extends to operational efficiency. For example, manufacturing companies use AI to predict imminent equipment failures. This way, manufacturers can conduct preventative maintenance and reduce downtime from hardware failure while saving money on repairs.

Behind the scenes, AI employs sophisticated algorithms to detect patterns and correlations in data that humans are much more likely to miss. It doesn't replace human decision-makers but boosts their ability to make well-informed choices. Machine learning models improve over time, continuously learning from new data to refine their predictions and recommendations.

AUTOMATION OF ROUTINE TASKS

Automating routine tasks is probably one of the first things you think about when you hear the words 'artificial intelligence.' A mountain of data entry work is disappearing because AI has taken over these tasks in one fell swoop. AI, such as optical character recognition technologies, have evolved considerably over the years, with AI now able to read documents, extract relevant information, and input it directly into databases with astonishing accuracy. While OCR has been around for many years, it's only with AI that it can handle nearly any physical document, no matter its state of preservation. If any pieces of text are harder to read, blurry, or washed out, AI can make informed guesses about the content and transcribe it accordingly. It can also easily detect a document's language and script. With this technology, companies save hours of manual work, reduce human error, and keep data up to date. The main benefit is that AI doesn't just scan but understands the text it scans. These systems can now categorize emails, sort forms, and manage invoices, making paper trails a thing of the past.

Customer service is getting a facelift with AI-powered chatbots that can handle inquiries 24/7. These aren't the clunky, confusing bots of yesteryear but sophisticated systems using natural language processing to understand and respond to customer questions and requests accurately. They can answer FAQs, process orders, handle complaints, and interpret issues. However, human customer service reps are still available for more complex issues. This shift reduces wait times and improves overall satisfaction.

Furthermore, if you're drowning in emails, AI is here to help. Email filters have become smarter and are able to put forth important messages and flag spam much more accurately than ever before. Some systems also offer predictive responses, making replying to emails a breeze. This technology learns from your email habits to keep your inbox tidy and manageable without constant vigilance.

Coordinating meetings across different time zones and schedules can feel like a logistical nightmare. That's because it is. But AI scheduling assistants are taking the pain out of scheduling. They can find optimal meeting times for all parties involved and then send out invites and reminders to everyone. Automation eliminates the back-and-forth emails that scheduling often entails, freeing up time for actual work.

Businesses and influencers alike must maintain an active social media presence to stay afloat. But this can be incredibly time-consuming, especially if you don't have a considerable PR team behind you. AI tools now analyze engagement data to determine the best times to post and suggest content likely to perform well. Some platforms even automate posting across various channels for a consistent and strategic online presence without the need for daily oversight.

In retail and manufacturing, AI does inventory management better than humans could hope to. By analyzing sales data, seasonal trends, and supply chain logistics, AI can predict stock levels, automate reordering processes, and optimize warehouse organization. It prevents stockouts and overstocking and reduces the need for manual stock checks, saving countless hours and significantly reducing waste.

In production lines, AI visual inspection systems detect defects or inconsistencies in products at a speed and accuracy level far beyond human capability. These systems learn from thousands of images what a perfect product should look like and can identify even the slightest deviations so that only items meeting the highest quality standards reach customers with lower error rates and fewer returns.

Similarly, financial institutions and legal firms have to deal with the verification of documents. It's a process that can be tedious and prone to errors if done by humans. AI systems now verify the authenticity of documents, check for compliance, extract, and then organize information for easy access. AI-imbued verification is faster and boosts security and compliance. Document integrity is paramount in these sectors, so any way to reduce error and improve security is always a good thing.

Businesses with a mobile workforce must manage travel arrangements and expenses, which can be a logistical challenge. AI tools automate much of this by taking over tasks like booking flights and accommodations depending on personal preferences and corporate policies or categorizing expenses and flagging potential fraud. It simplifies travel planning and expense reporting for employees and provides opportunities for cost savings.

In industries that rely on heavy machinery, such as manufacturing, transportation, and energy, AI predicts when equipment might fail or need maintenance. By analyzing data from sensors that monitor machine performance, AI can identify patterns that precede a breakdown so producers can schedule maintenance on time. This is called predictive maintenance. It reduces downtime, extends the lifespan of equipment, and can significantly reduce the money spent on maintaining equipment compared to reactive maintenance.

AI in education is making learning as unique as every student's favorite playlist. It's keeping tabs on how students tackle problems, what grabs their attention, and how fast they're able to go through lessons. Then, it adjusts their learning material, making it just right for them. Artificial intelligence is a learning aid that knows exactly when you're ready for the next level or when to switch gears and try a different way of learning something challenging. This means students are learning it in a way that sticks because their teaching has been custom-fitted for their learning style, time, and attention.

AI is big in the creative pool, too, as mentioned earlier. It can create catchy marketing blurbs and eye-catching designs quickly. These tasks count as repetitive since companies have to create large volumes of these often. With AI ideas and rough drafts, the creative process is getting a boost. You still have to add a human touch, of course, but AI helps with ideas, brainstorming sessions, and making previously time-consuming drafts. Some are gold, and some might need a bit of polishing, but it all helps improve creativity.

CHAPTER 5

TACKLING COMMON MISCONCEPTIONS ABOUT AI

There's a fascinating crossroads where technology meets society in dramatic ways, particularly in work. AI and automation paint a picture of a future where machines take away the tasks many people dread, leaving behind more time for creativity, innovation, and perhaps a bit of leisure. But there's a flip side to it—the fear of job displacement, a concern as old as technology itself. It's a valid concern. After all, this isn't the first time humanity has faced this challenge, and it is unlikely to be the last.

However, to see the bright side, think of a workday full of engaging activities that play to your strengths, creativity, and emotional intelligence—qualities that are quintessentially human. This is a potential reality in an AI-augmented workplace.

Meanwhile, there is a call to slow down a little with how much society might be leaning on AI. It's easy to wonder if we're getting somewhat too cozy with letting AI make decisions. AI may be less likely to make errors than humans in some aspects, but it is far from perfect. It takes critical thinking and paying close attention to what to accept and what to bring into question when engaging with AI feedback and suggestions.

JOB DISPLACEMENT

It's no secret that automation and AI can perform tasks that were traditionally a human-only job. Self-checkout kiosks and software automating routine office tasks and many other examples are already common. Studies, such as one by McKinsey, suggest that by 2030, up to 30% of the current work hours globally could be automated. However, this doesn't mean a direct loss of jobs but a shift in the type of work that humans might do. Job displacement doesn't necessarily equate to job elimination but rather a transformation of one job into another. However, the concern is entirely valid because whenever a new technology emerges, not everyone can keep up with the change and adapt in time. Moreover, companies aren't always willing to adapt gradually, especially within certain industries or work cultures.

This is where it gets interesting, however. History shows that technological advancements, while disrupting existing job markets, also pave the way for new opportunities. The rise of the World Wide Web is a prime example. It has automated many tasks but also spawned roles that were unfathomable a few decades ago—think app developers, social media managers, and digital content creators. AI and automation are no different. They're likely to birth new industries and jobs, especially in AI development, data analysis, and cybersecurity, to name a few. The World Economic Forum predicts that by 2025, 97 million new jobs may appear that combine the new division of labor between humans, machines, and algorithms into new, integrated roles.

One of the most constructive responses to the changing job market is not to panic but to reskill and upskill. Routine tasks are increasingly more automated, and that's generally a good thing. However, with this comes a growing demand for skills that AI can't replicate—genuine creativity, emotional intelligence, complex problem-solving, philosophical approaches, and coming up with entirely new concepts. There's also prompt engineering as an example of a new type of job never seen before. Lifelong learning and adapting education systems to focus on these skills can prepare the workforce for an AI-augmented future with less worry about displacement or job insecurity. Luckily, many companies and governments are already tackling reskilling programs head-on.

As AI starts reshaping jobs, a big role emerges for rules and support to help everyone land on their feet when the AI revolution comes for their roles. It's important to create both a safety net and a plan for the future that accounts for worker's rights and circumstances. That doesn't just mean keeping jobs but also maintaining respectable pay and keeping up with prices and inflation. New job opportunities must allow everyone to get a fair share of the pie, not just the tech-savvy individuals and early adopters who already know how to leverage the technology.

Exploring how AI shakes things up in different jobs is like looking through a prism—each industry refracts the impact differently. For example, in manufacturing, AI and robotics are making things faster and more efficient while also changing the kind of skills that are in demand. They shift the spotlight toward those who can synchronize with these machines, keep them running, and fix them when they act up. Flip the script to the creative sectors, and AI's role is more of a muse than a maestro, despite the initial impression of AI art as a replacement. Rather, it sparks new ideas, often rough and unrefined ones, helps writers out of their blocks, and gives artists a new palette to play with. Healthcare, too, is feeling the AI breeze, with algorithms sifting through data to spot diagnoses quicker, which in turn lets healthcare professionals spend more quality time with patients. In any of these cases, the human touch remains irreplaceable.

The job scene is changing everywhere, but not in the same way. Tech-forward regions might show much more excitement overall, riding the wave of new opportunities and innovations. Meanwhile, areas that have traditionally leaned on sectors more prone to automation might be more anxious and feel threatened as they ponder what the future holds. Therefore, strategies that play to each area's strengths and challenges can make the AI transition more palatable for everyone and less painful economically, socially, culturally, or in any other way.

The gig economy's entanglement with AI advancements adds another layer to the plot. It's creating new kinds of gigs, unsurprisingly, but it is also sparking conversations about what job security looks like. That's especially true when work becomes a series of gigs rather than a 9-to-5. The gig economy itself has been controversial and revolutionary at the same time. It has the potential for innovation but also asks for dialogue on rights and protections for those in ever-flexible yet uncertain terrain.

Public perception and AI literacy are the secrets to making this transition smoother. If people understand what AI can (and can't) do, how it works, see its potential beyond the sci-fi scenarios, and grasp the opportunities it brings, then an AI-integrated job market feels less like a leap into the unknown and more like stepping into a future brimming with possibilities.

So, here's a thought to ponder. As AI nudges some jobs to the side, it also pushes new business dreams and ventures. AI creates room for fresh startups and ideas that could light up the job market in ways you haven't even dreamed of yet.

DEPENDENCE RISKS

It's clear that AI is deeply permeating daily lives, work, entertainment, communication, and even basic home appliances. It's moving at break-neck speeds, and humanity is entrusting AI with critical decisions in areas such as autonomous vehicles and healthcare systems. However, there's a risk. One that is at once glaringly obvious and hidden in plain sight. A glitch or misjudgment by AI could lead to safety concerns. And relying too much on AI means missing these mistakes due to blind trust. For example, an autonomous car misinterpreting a stop sign due to a smudge could have serious, even lethal, consequences. To mitigate these risks, there's a need for rigorous testing, continuous learning models that adapt and improve, and, importantly, keeping a human in the loop for oversight and ethical decisions.

AI is now welcome in homes and businesses, but it's also opening the door to potential security vulnerabilities. AI systems, like any other technology, can be susceptible to hacking and misuse. Picture an AI security camera system being tricked by sophisticated hackers who potentially also use AI to trick or 'poison' another AI. One solution (or mitigation) is robust encryption, along with regular software updates, to stay ahead of threats. AI systems also must have security in mind from the point of initial conception.

AI has a bit of a curiosity streak. It often demands vast amounts of data to learn and make informed decisions. This can put privacy under a magnifying glass, with AI systems potentially knowing everything from their users' shopping habits to their preferred route to work. Not only is this a little unsettling from an ethical standpoint, particularly regarding consent, but it also could mean this data is vulnerable to falling into the wrong hands. The balance is to implement strict data protection regulations, like GDPR in Europe, to keep data as anonymous as possible and give users control over their data. Transparency about how data is used builds trust and keeps the magnifying glass at a respectful distance.

Relying on AI for everything from choosing what to watch next to making business decisions could lead to a sort of digital dependency, where critical thinking takes a backseat to letting the bot do all the work. To avoid this, users need to keep in mind (and be educated on) digital literacy and critical thinking skills. After all, AI is a tool, not a crutch, and decision-making should be informed by AI but not dictated by it.

These risks aren't just a job for tech wizards behind the scenes to solve. Instead, everyone, from policymakers to end-users, has to play a part. Education on digital ethics, a push for transparent AI practices, and the promotion of a culture of security and privacy can all contribute to a safer, more secure AI-integrated future.

A less talked about but equally critical risk of over-reliance on AI is the amplification of existing bias. Humans are naturally biased creatures. It's hard to avoid, as recognizing patterns and putting everything we learn or encounter into categories is a byproduct of how our brains work. While it's helpful when these categories or 'boxes' are true or at least close enough to the truth, it also opens up room for misunderstanding, over-application, bias, and presumptions. Since AI learns from humans, it also picks up on our unconscious bias. AI systems learn from historical data, and if that data contains bias or limited information, AI can perpetuate or even exacerbate these issues.

For example, AI used in recruitment might unfairly favor certain demographics due to biased historical hiring data. Combating this requires diversity in the data and in the teams developing AI, along with the implementation of fairness metrics and audits so AI can treat all users ethically and without unintentionally discriminating against some. And, of course, that means not using AI only when making decisions about living, breathing humans.

With over-reliance on AI, there's a real worry it could leave some individuals behind, widening the gap between the tech-savvy and those less so. A world where only a handful have the latest technology and know-how while others are left in the corner isn't exactly appealing. That's the digital divide. To bridge this gap, everyone must be on board just enough—from tech giants to governments—to make AI tools and the knowledge to use them spread far and wide.

Then there's the concern that leaning too heavily on AI could start to impact our thought processes and how we connect with each other. If you ever found yourself doom-scrolling on social media, courtesy of AI nudging you to click just one more video, or realized you're only seeing news that echoes your own views, it's thanks to algorithms. The bubble effect can skew an individual's view of the world and even negatively impact their mental health. The fix is promoting digital well-being, creating AI that nudges toward good habits, and making sure we still have plenty of real human interactions.

Peering into the future, AI is undoubtedly going to be a part of the everyday world in gadgets, smart homes, and online. But more importantly, it's also going to shape culture, ethics, and how we people understand intelligence. While humanity builds and grows with AI, it must be in a way that reflects the best values and brings everyone along for the ride. This means having open conversations about where AI is heading and steering it toward doing good for all, not just a select few, but without crippling or censuring it, potentially taking away its creative edge.

And since AI doesn't stop at borders, tackling its challenges can't either. It's a global task that requires countries, international entities, companies, and communities to link arms and work together. It means setting up shared rules, being clear about how AI is used, and sharing its perks and powers evenly.

AI VS. ROBOTICS

AI is, first and foremost, what you find in software. It's the brainpower behind the scenes, crunching numbers, learning from data, and making decisions based on patterns. AI is the smart part of your computer or phone that can learn, adapt, and sometimes even outsmart human brains in specific tasks. It's what powers your favorite voice assistants, recommendation engines on Netflix, or uncannily accurate photo tagging on social media.

Robots, on the other hand, are about hardware. They're the physical, sometimes clunky, sometimes sleek machines that move, sense, and interact with the physical world. When you picture a robot, think of the Mars rovers exploring alien terrains, automated arms assembling cars in factories, or the vacuum cleaners that scare your cat. Robots can be as simple as a mechanical arm or as complex as humanoid robots trying to mimic human actions.

So, where does the confusion come in? It's when these two worlds collide. A robot becomes a lot more interesting if and when it's powered by AI. That's when you get robots that can navigate through a room, avoiding obstacles (and pets), or those that can learn to pick up objects they've never encountered before. This combination is where the merging of different technologies happens, combining the physical capabilities of robots with the smart decision-making prowess of AI. But keep in mind that not all AI has a physical form, and not all robots are smart on their own—it's the AI software that gives them a bit of that 'brain.' Yet, this combination, while perhaps the most traditional idea of a robot, is, in truth, still the rarest.

However, AI's capabilities are vastly expanding. Artificial intelligence is becoming adept at teaching a robot to get around a room intelligently while also developing algorithms that can diagnose diseases from medical images or predict weather patterns more accurately than ever before. These tasks rely purely on AI's ability to analyze and learn from data without any need for a robot's helping hand.

On the flip side, consider the advancements in robotics without AI. These machines can perform pre-programmed tasks with incredible precision and speed, essential in industries like manufacturing and logistics. However, without AI, their abilities to adapt to new situations or learn from their environment are limited. It's like having a super-efficient worker who can't deviate from the script. The moment you introduce AI into the equation, these robots go from following a strict playbook to improvising, learning, and improving their performances over time of their own accord. This synthesis of AI and robotics is paving the way for breakthroughs in autonomous vehicles, where the car itself is the robot, and AI is the driver, making split-second decisions using real-world data.

AI ERRORS AND WHY AI ISN'T PERFECT

One truth about AI stands firm even as it becomes more and more sophisticated: it is not perfect. Sure, it's already incredibly smart and can do some amazing things that were hard to imagine not long ago. But just like humans, AI can make mistakes, too. It's good to be aware of these errors to manage your expectations and use AI within its (admittedly ever-changing) limits.

First off, AI learns from data, and sometimes that data isn't perfect. If the information fed into an AI system has errors or biases, the AI will likely pick those up and make mistakes. Think of it like teaching a child – if you teach them something wrong, they'll repeat that mistake until (and if) they learn otherwise. For example, if an AI system is trained on historical hiring data that contain biases, it might end up making biased hiring recommendations.

Another reason AI can mess up is that it relies heavily on patterns. It's great at recognizing patterns in data, but it can struggle when something unexpected comes up. Let's say an AI is trained to recognize dogs in photos. Show it a weirdly dressed dog or a dog partially hidden, and it might get confused. This is because AI doesn't understand context the way humans do, at least not yet. Instead, it sees data in black and white.

There's also the issue of overfitting. Overfitting happens when an AI model learns the training data too well, including all the noise and exceptions. In a way, the machine memorizes a textbook rather than understands the material. It will perform great on the training data but might struggle with new, unseen data. If you were like the AI and only studied the questions you know will be on a test and then got a trick question you didn't prepare for, the struggle would be similar.

Then, there are simple glitches and bugs. While the way they work may feel substantially different than traditional programs, at the end of the day, AI systems are made up of complex algorithms and code, much like your operating system, for one. And just like with any other program, sometimes things go wrong. Even the tiniest error in the code can lead to unexpected behavior due to the domino effect of bugs. After all, AI is created by humans, and humans aren't perfect, either.

Lastly, AI lacks common sense. While it can process and analyze massive amounts of data faster than any human, it doesn't have the innate understanding of the world that humans do. It might seem to have common sense, thanks to its vast knowledge. However, once you see it make seemingly absurd mistakes that no human would, such as assuming two things are inherently linked because they often appear together, you will realize that it's an illusion. So, the AI might make decisions that seem logical based on data but are completely off-base in real life.

AI IN EVERYDAY LIFE, DISPELLING SCI-FI MYTHS

When most people think of AI, they might imagine scenes straight out of a sci-fi movie: robots taking over the world, computers with human-like consciousness, and all kinds of futuristic strangeness. But the reality of AI in everyday life is way more down-to-earth and way less dramatic. Let's clear up some of those sci-fi myths and see how AI is actually working for us in practical, helpful ways.

Let's briefly touch on smart assistants like Siri, Alexa, and Google Assistant once more. These AI helpers aren't plotting world domination; they're here to make your life a bit easier (when they work as intended, at least). They can set reminders, play your favorite music, give you weather updates, and even tell you a joke. They're pretty smart, but they're not sentient beings with secret agendas—they're advanced tools that respond to your voice commands.

That said, while they may not be the kind of threat sci-fi movies might promise, it doesn't mean there aren't potential concerns to be aware of. Since they are connected to the Internet and trained on your voice and routine, there is a potential for security and privacy risks. Moreover, there are ethical concerns with giving so much of your data and depending on virtual assistants. There are times when the good old pen and paper might be the best for keeping track of your sensitive activities, and a physical switch might be best for your lights or thermostat.

AI is also a big player in online shopping. Sites like Amazon use AI to suggest products you might like using your past purchases and browsing history. It's like having a personal shopper who knows your tastes and can help you find what you're looking for quickly. Again, no magic or mind-reading here—just smart algorithms doing their thing.

However, once more, having corporations and websites track your habits extensively may not be ideal for your privacy. Meanwhile, scams involving online shopping are catching up on these trends and may try to exploit your habits to get to your sensitive banking information.

Let's not forget about the AI in smartphones, from facial recognition that unlocks your phone to predictive text that guesses what you're going to type next. These features make using your phone more convenient and secure, but they're not out to get you. The phone won't make decisions for you or try to exploit you. However, you should still be mindful about what permissions you give to which software. It may not be a sci-fi mastermind, but your phone can listen, see, and keep track of much of your daily activities. It likely also holds sensitive info, such as your bank account details.

In the realm of home automation, AI is helping to make living spaces more comfortable and efficient. Smart thermostats like Nest learn your schedule and adjust the temperature accordingly, saving energy and money. Smart lights can turn on and off based on your habits, and even smart refrigerators can keep track of what you're running low on. AI makes life a little bit easier, not taking over your home. However, just as with any other form of AI or IoT, don't rely on it too much. If anything breaks down or otherwise stops working as it should, the trusty old manual and mechanical installations are a good backup.

Healthcare is another area where AI is making a real difference. From apps that help you track your fitness and diet to algorithms that assist doctors in diagnosing diseases, AI is boosting the ability to take care of yourself. These tools provide support and insights, but they're not replacing human doctors—they're just adding an extra layer of assistance.

So, while AI might seem like something out of a sci-fi movie, its role in our daily lives is much more practical and helpful. No killer robots or dystopian futures here—just smart tools designed to help us out. But it is true that these tools can be misused. However, so long as you rely on that standout human capability and common sense, you should be all right.

TACKLING MISCONCEPTIONS ABOUT AI SAFETY AND SECURITY

Let's talk about AI safety and security. There's plenty of noise around AI, and with it, there is a fair share of misconceptions. Some people think AI is going to lead to all sorts of scary scenarios, but let's break it down and get to the real story.

Before talking about misconceptions about the danger of AI, it's worth addressing the assumptions about its safety. One common misconception is that AI systems are always secure and infallible. Just like any other technology, AI can have vulnerabilities. For example, just as a smartphone can get hacked, so can AI systems if they're not properly protected. Remember that AI isn't some invincible force. It's built on software that needs updates, user awareness, and security checks.

On the exact opposite end of the security misconception spectrum, people also worry about AI being used for malicious purposes, like cyber-attacks. While it's true that any technology can be misused, the same AI that could potentially be used for hacking can also be used to defend against such threats. AI can identify and respond to security breaches much faster than humans can, making our digital world safer. It's a bit of a cat-and-mouse game, but AI is a powerful tool on the side of the good, too.

Then there's the fear of AI spying on people. Yes, it is true that AI systems can collect data, and using AI (or IoT or similar tools) for intrusive activities is a realistic concern. However, many companies and governments are working on rules to protect user privacy and mandate the ethical use of AI. That may not be entirely reassuring to everyone, but it is a significant step. Still, be aware of what data you share and try to use services that respect your privacy. Just like you wouldn't share your personal information with a shady website, you need to be smart about how you interact with AI.

Some people think AI will make humans obsolete in security roles. In reality, AI is more likely to assist rather than replace, especially in security. For example, AI can monitor security cameras and flag suspicious activity, but human security professionals still need to check and act on those alerts. It's about teamwork—AI handles the heavy lifting of monitoring, and humans make the critical decisions.

Lastly, there's the idea that AI will run amok without proper regulations. The truth is that many experts are already working on creating guidelines and frameworks to develop and use AI responsibly. It's a collaborative effort involving researchers, governments, and industries to make sure AI benefits everyone and doesn't get out of hand.

THE AI DECISION-MAKING MYTHS

Recently, there's a bit of a myth that AI is making all the decisions for us and taking control. But the reality is a lot less dramatic. AI is much more involved with decision-making, but humans are still very much in control.

AI is great at crunching numbers, spotting patterns, and making predictions from data. One example is that AI can help doctors diagnose diseases by analyzing medical records and imaging. But here's the thing: AI doesn't make the final call. Doctors use the information AI provides to make informed decisions, combining their expertise with the insights AI offers.

Another example is in business. AI can analyze market trends and suggest strategies, but it's up to human managers to decide what actions to take. AI might recommend which products to stock based on sales data, but the final decision rests with the people who understand the nuances of their business and customers. AI provides the tools, but humans apply the wisdom. That means humans don't accept the suggestions blindly or without double-checking, and they have every right to refuse or ignore them.

In everyday life, think about the recommendations you get from streaming services like Netflix or Spotify. AI suggests movies and music by learning your preferences, but you're the one who decides what to watch or listen to. It's a helpful nudge, not a command. Chances are, you might not even like what it suggests. In that case, you can make the suggestion as unhelpful to guide the AI toward better recommendations.

There's also the myth that AI will completely take over decision-making roles like hiring and firing employees. While AI can assist in sorting through resumes and identifying potential candidates, human recruiters and managers still conduct interviews and make the final hiring decisions. AI can streamline the background hurdles of hiring, but it doesn't replace the human judgment necessary to understand if someone is a good fit for the company or not.

And let's talk about self-driving cars. While AI helps these cars navigate and make split-second decisions on the road, there's always a human element involved in the oversight and regulation of these systems. Even in fully autonomous vehicles, humans are designing the safety protocols and response strategies.

One of the biggest misconceptions is that AI can operate and make choices without any human input. In reality, AI systems need continuous monitoring and updating. Engineers and data scientists are always tweaking algorithms, feeding in new data, and making adjustments to make AI work correctly and safely.

Also, consider the ethical decisions. AI doesn't have morals or values. Some of its responses (or refusals) might make it seem like it does, but ultimately, it's just a tool with some digital guardrails attached. Humans are the ones who set the guidelines and boundaries for how AI should be used. This means making sure AI applications align with ethical standards and societal values or helping them discern nuance and gray areas.

CHAPTER 6

ETHICAL CONSIDERATIONS AND AI

Living in the digital age means that personal data is now a form of currency. In every click, like, and share, there's a slice of a person interacting with the digital world, ripe for the picking by AI systems that learn from habits, preferences, and even quirks. The intersection of technology and privacy is a modern crossroads, one where the excitement of innovation meets the cautionary tale of personal space invasion.

The conversation around privacy also covers autonomy, respect, and the right to engage with the cyber world on your own terms. Privacy shouldn't mean shunning innovation for fear of exposure but demanding a future where technology and privacy meet on equal grounds, respectful of each other's boundaries.

Furthermore, AI, a mirror reflecting the data it's fed, can sometimes also show the uncomfortable truth. It's the truth about biases that are sometimes so deeply ingrained that it's almost impossible to recognize them. AI has to respect privacy and be as unbiased and equitable as the users it is supposed to support and uplift. Fighting bias must happen both through varied data and diverse teams working on the development and management of artificial intelligence.

PRIVACY CONCERNS

Data in the era of AI is the new gold rush, with tech giants and startups alike mining for this precious resource—sometimes transparently, other times not so much. With great data comes great responsibility, especially in terms of privacy.

At the heart of many AI systems is a voracious appetite for data. The more data AI has, the smarter it gets. The way it acquires this data could be by analyzing your shopping habits, your favorite travel destinations, posts on social media, or your facial expressions. When you get those eerily accurate product recommendations while browsing online, that's AI working in the background with data, having learned your preferences better than a best friend might. But there is a catch, and a big one at that. If not managed carefully, data collection can cross into the territory of privacy invasion, turning personalized experiences into privacy concerns or even risks of exploitation by bad actors like identity thieves.

Take into account smart speakers that can order pizza, play your favorite tunes, or control home lighting with just a voice command. They're always listening, ready to act as soon as you need them. While that's certainly convenient, it raises questions such as 'What happens to those recordings?', 'Who listens to them?' and 'How are they used?' Transparency about data usage and stringent safeguards are necessary so homes don't become open books for corporations, hackers, or worse, burglars.

Sharing data with AI systems can lead to innovations in healthcare, education, science, and safety. AI can predict health issues before they become serious, adjust learning to individual student's learning profiles, or make roads safer with autonomous driving tech. However, the dilemma is balancing these benefits with the need to protect individual privacy. Data needs to be as anonymous as possible, and users must give clear consent for data use. Users should also have control over their data.

Protecting privacy in the age of AI isn't just a job for the tech experts but a collective responsibility. Being informed about how our data is used, advocating for stronger privacy protections, and supporting companies that use AI responsibly and clearly are ways that we can all contribute to a future where AI benefits society without compromising privacy.

One way to make privacy better protected is to use decentralized data models, like the blockchain, for storing and processing personal data. Distributing data across a network rather than storing it in a central location makes it significantly harder for unwanted parties to access or misuse personal information.

This is a technique that adds 'noise' to data in a way that lets AI learn patterns without identifying individuals. It's like being able to study the forest's ecosystem without being able to pinpoint the location of any single tree. Differential privacy means that AI can be trained on vast datasets while preserving individual anonymity.

Another concept in AI is 'explainable AI,' also known as XAI. The purpose of XAI is to make the inner workings of artificial intelligence more transparent and comprehensible. In the past, AI models were often seen as enigmatic 'black boxes,' with their decision-making being a mystery to those using them. A lack of understanding can create distrust in the reliability of AI and also puts users at a greater risk of their data being used in a way they wouldn't consent to. Therefore, XAI uncovers how AI comes to its conclusions in order to build trust and confidence in its decision-making abilities and inner workings.

Another way to handle privacy is the concept of federated learning. It doesn't require the (often power-hungry) blockchain. Instead of sending your data to a central server for AI training, federated learning brings the AI algorithms to your device. Your data stays on your device, and only the learning—not the specific data points—gets shared with the world. It's akin to learning a dance move from a video without having to show anyone your awkward first attempts. This model of learning is particularly useful for sensitive applications like personal health monitoring.

Now, let's address the concept of privacy by design. This concept involves incorporating privacy protections into the very development of AI systems rather than as an afterthought. It means thinking about privacy at every stage of the AI lifecycle, from the first rough design to deployment and beyond. When privacy is baked into the tech, it's inherently more secure and trustworthy.

Keeping personal info safe in an ever more digital world isn't easy, but it's definitely something to get behind. Think about being in charge of your own digital shadow and having the know-how to manage who sees what about you online. Privacy settings must be crystal clear, understanding how others use your data must be as easy as a few clicks, and you must hold the reins over your digital trail.

Clear privacy policies and making it simple for people to say yes or no to how their data is used are like giving everyone the power to control their own digital footprint and feel safe as they leave a trail behind. But knowing is half the battle. Teaching people why they must keep their data under lock and key and how to actually do it is the other half.

This brings us back to laws like the EU's GDPR with regard to data protection. These laws set strict rules to make (or force) companies to keep user data safe, explain how they're using it, and let people have a say in the whole process. What if this kind of protection was the same everywhere? A worldwide agreement on keeping data safe would mean no matter where you are or where your data ends up. It will have the same ironclad protection.

BIAS AND FAIRNESS

When AI is in the spotlight, it's akin to stepping into a world where the line between human and machine intelligence blurs. AI, in many ways, is a reflection of the data we feed it, a mirror to the human world, warts and all. This mirroring is where the issues of bias and fairness sneak in, subtly yet significantly impacting the fairness of AI-driven decisions. The crux of the matter lies in the data. It is rich, diverse, vast, but sometimes flawed. If the data reflects historical or other biases, AI, in its quest to learn, may inadvertently perpetuate these biases. Let's say you're learning to paint landscapes, but you're doing so from a book that only shows deserts. Your view of the world might become skewed, limited to sandy expanses. It's not intentional or even malicious, but it's hard to avoid when there's a limited perspective or knowledge.

Consider facial recognition technology. It's a marvel of AI that can recognize individuals in milliseconds. Yet, when the training data lacks exposure to enough different types of faces, its accuracy wanes, particularly for people of different ethnic backgrounds. This is a profound issue, even if it might not seem so at first glance. However, it could affect everything from security to personal rights to job prospects.

But here's where the narrative takes a hopeful turn. The fight against AI bias is robust and involves a multi-faceted approach to creating and propelling AI systems that are as unbiased as they are intelligent. It begins with the data—data that includes everything from any culture, group, subculture, sphere of interest, and sensitive subject. It's a means of understanding and representing the wealth of human experience in a way that stays true to reality, at least as closely as possible.

Equally significant is the composition of the teams that work on AI development. Variety in thought, background, skill, education, and perspective among developers is a safeguard against unconscious bias. When enough different human experiences go into it, the AI that comes out of this development will be equitable and accurate.

Then there's the push for transparency. AI, for all its complexity, can no longer be a black box. Understanding how and why decisions are made leads to the discovery and correcting of these biases. Understandable and accountable AI means that if it ever does display bias, stereotype, or even confusion, it's easy to understand why it happens and how to go about the solution.

Crafting AI with a conscience isn't a one-shot deal. Instead, it's an ongoing adventure, constantly tweaking and learning to keep the emerging digital aides smart and morally sound. It involves creating a moral compass for AI and then keeping it on a path that's good for everyone, not just now but in the future. However, the trick and trouble is keeping this moral compass fair and neutral. Without ethical considerations, there is a risk of creating AI that is hardly useful and potentially discriminatory or even dangerous. However, too much restriction could lead to censorship and different kinds of bias, plus a potential drawback for researchers, theoreticians, and storytellers exploring controversial or touchy subjects.

Think about who's building this AI. It shouldn't just be the brainiacs in tech hubs and labs calling the shots. Everyone should have a say, especially folks who don't usually get to be in the room where it happens. Bringing in diverse voices means we can spot the stuff that might not work for everyone and fix it before it becomes a problem. It's like making sure the whole crew is on board and in agreement on where the ship's headed.

Now, onto learning about AI. It might be easier to learn how to use it than to understand the big picture—considerations such as why AI decides who gets a job interview and who doesn't can be complex. Education about AI, from the playground to the boardroom, means everyone is better equipped to steer AI in the right direction.

Fairness and bias are global issues, and they manifest differently everywhere in the world. What's fair in one place might not cut it in another, and vice versa. However, settling for the lowest common denominator is not an option either, as it risks severely restricting those who wouldn't otherwise be affected. That's why it's necessary to communicate, share ideas, and work across borders. Another idea is to develop AI that is more private and adjustable for each user. For example, certain types of content may not be appropriate for all audiences, but it doesn't mean they are unethical in the right hands, which is something AI development must take into account.

AI and its role in everyday lives is growing by the minute, so the approach to keeping it ethical has to grow too. It's like updating the software to keep up with new issues and challenges. But for AI, it means updating both the software itself and the rules and regulations around it.

Therefore, keeping AI on the straight and narrow means setting up ground rules. And setting those rules is a team effort—tech pioneers, governments, and everyone in between need to pitch in. These rules are there to guide it so that as AI evolves, it includes everyone in a way that is respectful but also neutral, fair, and unbiased.

AI AND MEDIA

When you take a closer look at AI-driven personalization in media, you're looking at a double-edged sword that's as fascinating as it is controversial. On one hand, it's an unquestionable goldmine for entertainment. It becomes a personal DJ, newsreader, and movie critic all rolled into one, filling your digital feed with things you love or are likely to love. That's quite neat and even a time-saver. But here's the other side of the coin: this personalization isn't just shaping what we consume for fun; it's also shaping our views, opinions, and, ultimately, the decisions we make, including those at the ballot box.

AI personalization works by tracking clicks, likes, shares, and the time you spend on articles or videos. It then feeds this data into complex algorithms that figure out what you're most interested in. The result is a perfectly tailored news feed or video playlist. More importantly, AI doesn't forget or get it wrong after the third recommendation, for better or worse.

Consequently, this AI-curated content bubble can sometimes turn into an echo chamber, reinforcing existing beliefs without exposing people to differing viewpoints. This is where the democracy bit comes in. A well-functioning democracy thrives on informed citizens exposed to a broad range of ideas and perspectives. If we're only fed news and opinions that align with our existing beliefs, we're at risk of becoming less open to dialogue and compromise—key ingredients of democratic societies.

There's also the issue of misinformation. AI doesn't exactly 'know' what information it possesses but rather distills it into numbers, and sensational or controversial content often gets more engagement. This means algorithms might inadvertently prioritize and spread misinformation because it's just doing its job: keeping users engaged. It's not that AI is trying to meddle in democracy; it's just that in its given task to personalize content, it doesn't always distinguish between accurate information and clickbait.

Moreover, the definition of what misinformation is and isn't can also be murky. In anything cultural or societal, truth isn't bound by the strict rules of the scientific method as physics or pure logic may be. Instead, it comes in many shades of gray and differing perspectives. Artificial intelligence may do its best to remain neutral and purely logical, but sometimes, this isn't enough. Furthermore, while it is possible (and often encouraged) to have human evaluators analyzing and reporting on misinformation and guiding AI, the issue then goes back to human bias and limitations. These limitations then transfer to the AI in a potentially perpetual cycle.

But it's not all so gloomy. Awareness is the first step toward gaining informed opinions that are as close to the truth as possible. As users become savvier about how AI shapes media consumption, they can seek out varying sources from different narratives, question the information presented, and use AI to their advantage. Imagine AI that promotes media literacy, highlights diverse perspectives, and flags misinformation whenever possible and reasonable. We might be on the cusp of that reality, with developers and researchers working on more ethically aware AI systems that uphold the values of open debate and truth.

AI AND WARFARE

Here is another less discussed but interesting (and unnerving) ethical concern regarding the development of advanced artificial intelligence. AI and warfare take us into a dimension where the lines between science fiction and military reality blur. The use of AI in developing sophisticated weapons systems marks a seismic shift in warfare, introducing a future where decisions of immense consequence might be delegated to algorithms.

At the heart of this evolution is the development of autonomous weapons, often dubbed 'killer robots.' These might sound just like sci-fi movie androids, but they are actually drones, tanks, and naval vessels equipped with AI capable of identifying, tracking, and engaging targets without human intervention. The precision and efficiency they could potentially exhibit are undeniable, but so are the ethical quandaries they pose. Imagine a drone patrolling conflict zones, its AI sifting through data to decide whether to strike. The accountability for its actions—a core ethical concern—becomes murky. Who bears the responsibility if an autonomous weapon errs, causing unintended casualties? And what if it wasn't an error at all but a calculated intent of those behind guiding the AI?

Then there's the potential for an AI arms race as nations vie to outdo each other in military AI capabilities. The risk here isn't just about creating an imbalance of power but also the possibility of such technology falling into the wrong hands. Sophisticated AI weapons in the arsenal of rogue states or non-state actors could rewrite the rules of engagement, making it harder to maintain peace and security.

Moreover, AI's role in cyber warfare cannot be overlooked. AI algorithms can be wielded to penetrate defense networks, sabotage critical infrastructure, and spread misinformation, presenting a covert battlefield where the distinction between civilian and military targets blurs. Here, the ethical implications extend beyond the immediate impact, raising concerns about the erosion of privacy, freedom, and trust in the digital age.

The dialogue surrounding AI in warfare goes beyond the already complex debate about the ethical use of AI by individuals, companies, governments, and the military. It's also a matter of global norms and regulations to keep pace with technological advancements. It calls for an international consensus on the boundaries of AI in warfare, emphasizing the importance of maintaining human oversight and ethical considerations in the deployment of AI-powered weapons.

Reflecting on AI's role in warfare and weapon development brings to the fore the often-delicate balance between leveraging technology for national defense and upholding ethical standards that protect human dignity and rights. It's quite clear that the choices made today will shape the moral landscape of tomorrow's battlefields.

SURVEILLANCE CONCERNS

Surveillance isn't just about security cameras anymore. Today's AI-powered systems can analyze vast amounts of data in the blink of an eye. Governments and private and corporate entities are increasingly turning to AI to keep an eye on things, from monitoring traffic to spotting unusual behavior in crowded places. But this easily makes apparent a gnawing issue: as these AI systems become more common, so do concerns about privacy, consent, and the potential for misuse.

You could be walking down the street, knowing that AI systems are analyzing your every move and facial expression and possibly even trying to guess your mood. It sounds like something out of a dystopian sci-fi novel, but it's becoming more of a reality every day. This discussion is far from new, but the last decade has brought it into the light more severely and explicitly than ever before. With AI, the already highly sophisticated surveillance methods, like IoT devices potentially sending sensitive data to various entities, have taken a new form. These systems can identify individuals, track movements across a city, and possibly even predict people's actions, raising big questions about personal freedom and autonomy.

The ethical considerations around AI-driven surveillance are complex. On one hand, these systems can keep us safe, manage traffic more efficiently, and find missing persons faster than ever before. On the other hand, there's the risk of creating a society where everyone feels watched all the time. It's a bit like having a nosy neighbor who not only peeks over your fence but also takes notes and predicts what you'll do next weekend. It's entirely understandable that the more privacy-conscious individuals would see this development as something out of 1984 if taken too far.

Privacy is at the heart of the debate on AI surveillance. This isn't a matter of 'if you have nothing to hide, you have nothing to fear,' as privacy is deeply interconnected with consent and personal autonomy. The idea that someone—or something—might be recording and analyzing your every move without your consent is unsettling and unethical. Therefore, it's necessary to establish clear rules about what is and isn't acceptable in terms of surveillance and private data collection. This includes making people informed about when and how AI is watching and giving a legitimate, acceptable reason for it.

The main answers to all these concerns are transparency and accountability. If AI is going to be part of surveillance efforts, there must be systems in place to check what the AI is doing and why. There should be safeguards to prevent abuse and mechanisms for people to challenge decisions made by AI systems. After all, an AI system might not always get it right, and when it comes to something as important as surveillance, the stakes are high.

AI AND WORKERS' RIGHTS

Due to AI and automation becoming more entwined in the workplace, the gig economy is expanding like a giant balloon. Robots aren't just assembling cars or algorithms managing stock trades. The very nature of work is changing before our eyes. And with these changes, employment laws and labor rights are up for a major overhaul to maintain fairness and basic human rights in this brave new world.

The gig economy, powered by platforms like Uber, Upwork, Airbnb, and Freelancer, has created a world of opportunities for flexible, freelance work. Yet, this flexibility often comes without the safety net traditionally provided by full-time employment. In comes AI, the mastermind behind streamlining tasks and creating new job opportunities. However, the use of AI also raises questions about job security and workers' rights. It's like a game of musical chairs, where AI's tune could either add more chairs to the circle or take a few away.

Future employment laws will need to dance to the beat of this new tune. This means considering how to protect workers who might find themselves freelancing for an AI system. They must be fairly compensated and not overworked by the endless appetite of digital platforms. Employers must be aware that, while AI is a tool, it doesn't make work unrealistically easy, and a living wage matters. There must be a balance between leveraging AI for productivity and innovation and ensuring human workers aren't left in the dust.

Labor rights in the age of AI might include things like 'right to disconnect' laws to prevent burnout from always-on digital work environments or ensuring that gig workers have access to benefits and protections similar to those in traditional employment. There's also talk about 'AI fairness' to prevent automated systems from making biased hiring or firing decisions. It's all about drafting a playbook that keeps work fair, safe, and rewarding in an era where your co-worker might be a software program.

The future of work with AI needs to shape a society that values human dignity alongside progress. After all, we have to remember that behind every screen, app, and robot, there are people striving for a decent day's work and a fair day's pay. The laws and rights that evolve will reflect our collective vision for a future where technology serves humanity, not the other way around.

SUSTAINABILITY CONCERNS IN TRAINING AND RUNNING LARGE MODELS

When we think about AI, images of futuristic robots or smart devices might pop into our heads. But behind the scenes, these AIs are powered by massive, energy-hungry algorithms. Training large AI models is a bit like training an Olympic swimmer; just as athletes need pools, gyms, and tons of food, AI needs data centers and enormous amounts of electricity. The environmental footprint of these digital brains is significant, given the colossal amounts of computing power required to make them tick.

Recent studies have shed light on the carbon emissions generated by training some of the largest AI models. It turns out that bringing sophisticated AI to life can emit as much carbon as five cars over their lifetimes. That's a lot of carbon footprints for something that doesn't even have feet. This is partially because the data centers that power AI consume energy mainly from non-renewable sources, contributing to greenhouse gas emissions and global warming. Another reason is the way AI uses resources, needing large amounts of power-hungry graphical processing units (GPUs) to do the number-crunching. As AI becomes increasingly integral to our lives, the sustainability of its training processes is an urgent concern.

But it's not all doom and gloom. The researchers behind AI are putting considerable effort into greenifying AI. More efficient algorithms that require less computational horsepower to run and data centers using renewable energy sources like wind and solar are some of the solutions on the horizon. It's a future that intends to combine the best of technology with respect for our planet.

Another promising avenue is the optimization of AI algorithms for energy efficiency. Think of it as putting AI on a power diet, where algorithms are streamlined to do more with less energy. Researchers are also exploring new forms of hardware specially designed to run AI applications in a more energy-efficient manner. These aren't just pie-in-the-sky ideas; they're real, tangible innovations that could help mitigate the environmental impact of AI's insatiable appetite for power.

Addressing the environmental implications of AI means cutting down emissions and paving the way for a future where technology and sustainability go hand in hand. It's a challenge that calls for the brightest minds in tech, environmental science, and policy-making to come together. The ultimate goal is clear: to harness the transformative power of AI in a way that's kind to the planet.

AI AND HUMAN RIGHTS

Artificial intelligence and human rights is a fascinating topic that's both thrilling and unsettling. On the upside, AI has incredible potential to make life better. By "better", we don't simply mean making mundane tasks more futuristic. AI systems of the future have the potential to spot diseases early, create personalized learning plans, or help people understand their legal rights. Breakthroughs like these could bridge gaps and support underserved communities.

In some ways, AI could be the great equalizer. While it cannot replace a genuine human touch in any field, there are many things it can do for a fraction of the price of human labor. For example, it is often said that many brilliant minds exist on the margins, and the depth of their intellect and creativity may never be explored due to their social standing. However, with AI, someone with creative talent could offload some of the creative processes without the need to pay someone else.

Imagine a game developer from an economically disadvantaged background having an amazing, fresh idea for an indie game. However, while they may be a brilliant storyteller, coder, and perhaps even art designer who can create most of their own assets, they may not be able to compose music. Rather than giving up on the project because they cannot afford a composer, they can outsource music-making to an AI tool for a much lower price (or perhaps even for free).

But there's a darker side, too. AI can also threaten our rights if we're not careful. Picture surveillance systems powered by AI that track people without their consent—this is a huge privacy concern waiting to happen. Surveillance has already been a concern for many, especially with the growing presence of Internet-enabled devices everywhere. However, AI can amplify this issue beyond measure. In some places, facial recognition tech is being used to crack down on dissent and target disadvantaged, marginalized, or otherwise "undesirable" groups, which is a massive ethical problem.

There is also the possibility of either reducing or widening the digital divide. The digital divide is the gap between those who have easy access to technology and the Internet and those who don't. You may be familiar with it if you know about the adoption of television and personal computers (and later mobile phones and smartphones) around the world. It has not happened evenly everywhere. Personal computers have long been scarce in many parts of the world.

Still, interestingly enough, smartphones have taken over much faster and bridged the digital gap. However, this hasn't always been for the better, because people who jumped straight into the smartphone sphere may have missed out on significantly valuable tech skills that come from using a PC. This is an issue regarding AI as it has the potential to both widen and narrow the digital divide.

On one hand, AI has the potential to bridge the digital divide in that AI-powered tools can provide quality education to children in remote areas where good teachers are scarce. Healthcare can also improve with AI-driven diagnostics reaching places that lack medical professionals. These are huge boons for underprivileged communities.

But there's a flip side. If only people with money and resources are able to access the latest AI technologies, the divide will just get bigger. For example, in a situation where advanced AI is being used to automate jobs, only those on higher incomes may be able to afford to retrain and adapt. Meanwhile, others get left behind, stuck in low-paying jobs or left without any job at all. This situation would only increase inequality.

The way forward should be to make AI accessible to everyone. This means affordable Internet access, cheap but effective devices, and education programs that teach people how to use AI tools. It also involves creating AI systems that are easy to use, so you don't need a degree in computer science to benefit from them.

So, how do we harness the benefits of AI while avoiding the pitfalls? It really comes down to responsible AI usage. That means being transparent about how AI is applied, getting people's consent, and holding these systems accountable. It's also crucial to design AI that's unbiased and fair so it doesn't lead to discrimination.

On a global scale, we need consistent standards and regulations to protect human rights in the AI age. Governments, tech companies, and non-profits all have roles to play here. Governments can provide subsidies or incentives for tech infrastructure in underserved areas. Companies can design products with affordability and accessibility in mind. And non-profits can offer training and support to help people get up to speed with new technologies.

It's a complex challenge, no doubt. But if we get it right, AI could transform the world for the better in many exciting ways.

CHAPTER 7

HOW TO START INTEGRATING AI INTO YOUR DAILY LIFE

Having artificial intelligence be a part of your daily life might sound like a concept straight out of a sci-fi novel, but it's rapidly becoming a part of everyday reality. Smartphones, smart homes, you name it, AI is already woven into the fabric of daily routines, often in ways you might not even realize. This chapter will show you how to integrate AI into your daily life, making it easier, less intimidating, more efficient, and a bit more fun.

Artificial intelligence is a personal assistant that never sleeps, always knows your preferences, and is ready to help with everything from managing your schedule to suggesting what to cook for dinner. AI handles tasks that range from the mundane to the complex, so you have more time and energy for the things that matter more. With AI by your side, you can improve productivity at work, vary your entertainment options, stay fit and healthy, or have a non-judgemental and always-available talking partner when you need a venting ear. AI has something to offer everyone.

By the end of this chapter, you'll have a better understanding of how to find opportunities to use AI, get familiar with some of the best AI tools out there, and set realistic expectations about what AI can and can't do.

IDENTIFYING AI OPPORTUNITIES

AI is your digital sidekick ready to tackle tasks from the mundane to the mighty. You just have to look for a chance to use it. In fact, you might be using it already without even knowing, so check out your devices and gadgets for traces of AI. In personal contexts, AI might manage your calendar, suggest the best routes to beat traffic, or recommend a new series based on your binge-watching habits. For example, apps such as Google Assistant and Apple's Siri use AI to learn from your interactions, so they gradually become more helpful with each use. They remind you of appointments, tell you the weather, or control smart home devices. Then there's health-focused AI such as Fitbit's sleep tracker that analyzes your sleep patterns to give tips for better rest. If you have a health-focused smartwatch, that too might be interacting with AI to keep tabs on your health.

Beyond Fitbit's sleep tracker and health-focused smartwatches, there are other specific examples of AI health tools worth mentioning. Take smart blood pressure monitors—with BPM Connect and similar devices, AI can measure your blood pressure and sync the data to an app where you can track trends over time. These devices make it easier to keep an eye on your heart health and share accurate readings with your doctor if need be.

AI-powered apps can help those managing chronic conditions, too. For example, MySugr helps people with diabetes log their blood sugar levels, track their meals, and predict their A1C. It acts as a personal health assistant that helps you manage your condition day-to-day without constant guesswork.

Mental health is another area where AI tools are making a difference. Apps such as Wysa and Woebot offer support for mental well-being by providing a space to talk through your thoughts and feelings. These AI chatbots use cognitive-behavioral techniques (known as CBT) to help manage stress, anxiety, and other mental health challenges. Of course, they're not a replacement for professional help but can be a handy resource when you need to talk or get some advice.

In your professional life, AI likely already automates repetitive tasks for you. Tools like Zapier automate work by connecting a person's most-used apps and services. With tools like these, you delegate the boring bits to a virtual helper who never sleeps. Moreover, AI-driven platforms like Grammarly or Hemingway Editor can refine your writing, be it emails, reports, advertisements, or perhaps complaints. In this case, AI is a proofreader available 24/7 that never needs to rest or take a break.

But let's not forget about creativity in the workplace. AI tools such as Adobe's Sensei give you fascinating creative tools that automate the tedious parts of graphic design and video production so you can focus on unleashing your inner artist with a slightly lower barrier to entry. Or, even if you're a seasoned expert, you can use it to ensure your creativity won't be bogged down by the mundane parts of creative work.

Similarly, AI-driven data analysis tools crunch numbers in ways that would take humans hours, offering insights and patterns that can inform business strategies and decision-making.

So, it's clear that artificial intelligence can be used in numerous ways. But how do you spot opportunities to introduce AI to your day-to-day life? Start by identifying tasks that are repetitive or time-consuming, and then explore AI tools that can tackle these areas. Keep an eye on technology blogs and AI news platforms to stay updated on the latest tools and technologies.

If you handle large volumes of data at your job, AI can be a powerful ally for digging into big data that goes far beyond simple automation. For example, analytics tools like Tableau or PowerBI might let your company take advantage of large volumes of data quickly by finding trends and making predictions that inform strategic decisions. This means you can respond to market changes faster and more accurately.

In customer service, CRM systems such as Salesforce use AI during customer interaction to predict what customers might want and automate communications. Even though it's the AI doing it rather than a person, it makes these interactions more personal to each customer, which might make the customers happier and more willing to stick around.

On the personal side, if you want to make your life more convenient, manage your everyday tasks or health better, or automate things around you, there are so many opportunities to use AI. Let's say you want to live more healthily or manage health conditions. Advanced health trackers analyze your physical activity and biometric data to offer personalized health insights and recommendations. Or, AI can simply provide opportunities for you to live more comfortably. Home automation systems have developed to do more than just follow commands. They learn from your preferences to manage your home's security, energy usage, and more.

Perhaps you're a student or an avid lifelong learner. Coursera and Udemy, for example, use AI to suggest courses that can follow your pace and learning style. They adapt in real-time. This way, you can pick up information more easily. The AI will be present consistently, helping you learn, and you won't even notice it being there.

Money management can be a struggle, even for the number-savvy, but AI can lend a hand. Apps like Mint and YNAB are nifty—they can analyze your spending habits and offer smart tips to help you manage money more effectively. You don't have to guess where all your money's going. These apps will flag any unusual spending and suggest ways you can save.

And speaking of shopping, AI is practically everywhere in this realm. You might've already used an app like ShopSavvy. It uses artificial intelligence to scour the web and compare prices across different stores, and it lets you know when there are discounts. If you're looking for the best deal, especially during sale seasons, AI can find them for you.

For all the health enthusiasts out there, you might consider checking out AI-powered nutrition apps, such as MyFitnessPal or Noom, to name a few. They can take a look at your eating patterns and customize meal plans. The apps learn your preferences and goals so they can guide you toward making healthier choices without you having to think too hard about it.

As you can already tell, you often don't need to look for opportunities to use AI daily. It frequently finds its way to you. However, if you want to find opportunities to use it, look for tasks or decisions in your life that eat up time or could use an extra boost of insight. Staying on top of the latest AI advancements through tech news can also spark ideas for how this technology can make your life a little easier. Give it a try—you might be surprised at how much AI can do to simplify things.

SIMPLE AI TOOLS

After you realize how many opportunities there are to use AI regularly, you might want to get practical and try a few tools. However, some advanced AI tools may feel too complex and perhaps a little intimidating, especially if you aren't particularly tech-savvy. Luckily, there are plenty of user-friendly AI tools for beginners that can make daily life a bit easier, more organized, and a tad more fun without needing knowledge of code. Here's a look at some simple and accessible AI applications that you can start using today.

Let's start with organizing daily tasks. Todoist uses AI to help you manage your to-do list. Not only does it allow you to keep track of everything in one place, but it also suggests optimal dates for completing tasks based on your previous activity patterns. This personal assistant will know what you need even before you ask.

Next up are simple but incredibly convenient writing assistants like Grammarly and ProWritingAid. You don't have to be a professional author or journalist, nor do you need to know much about AI, to use them. These tools are a blessing for anyone who writes. It can be used in any writing, from emails to reports, authoritative articles, fictional stories, or even Facebook posts. While simple, they go beyond the spell-check function that your word processor may already have built-in. They use AI to improve your writing by checking for grammar errors, suggesting style improvements, and even evaluating the tone of your text.

Now, when you're feeling creative, you might feel like AI can't truly help the creative process or could be too advanced. DALL-E Mini, for example, is an AI program that generates images based on textual descriptions, isn't overstuffed with features, and needs virtually no complex skills to use. Just type in a phrase like "a two-headed flamingo" and watch as it brings your wildest imagination to visual life. This tool is fantastic for artists looking for inspiration or anyone curious to see how AI interprets creative prompts.

Besides Adobe's Sensei and DALL-E Mini, there are some other fantastic creative tools you should know about. Take Magisto as one more example. Magisto is an AI-driven video editing software that makes creating videos as smooth as butter. You just upload your footage, pick a style, and let Magisto do the rest. It edits your clips, adds music, and includes effects to give your video a polished look without you needing to spend hours tweaking it.

Then there's Canva, which has been around for a while but has recently become a go-to for anyone needing quick, stylish designs with a little help from AI. Canva's AI features can automatically suggest layouts, color schemes, and even design elements based on what you're creating. Whether working on social media posts, presentations, or invitations, Canva helps make your designs look professional with minimal effort.

Duolingo uses AI to offer personalized language learning. This app adapts its lessons based on how well you're doing, so you can practice in the areas where you need it most. Plus, it's gamified, which means you get to learn a new language while playing games. Learning Spanish, Japanese, and many other languages has never been more engaging.

Integrating AI into your home can be as simple as setting up smart speakers like Amazon Alexa or Google Home. These devices are pretty much plug-and-play. They use AI to learn from your routines and preferences to control your home's lighting, temperature, smart plugs, security systems, and more through simple voice commands. These voice commands aren't complex prompts or "magic spells" you must memorize. You simply have to speak naturally, as you would with another person, and the device will pick up on the request.

Now, imagine having a little helper in your pocket that not only manages your schedule but also keeps you calm and collected. That's exactly what simple AI assistant tools are here to do. ClickUp, for one, keeps your tasks in check and brings everything from your calendar to your project files into one place. Its AI feature breaks down complex information, making your day more organized and less stressful. Naturally, it'd be challenging to reduce stress through the use of AI if said AI tool was hard to use. That's why ClickUp and similar tools take very little time to learn, and once you do, it becomes second nature.

Then there's Cleo, a chatty AI assistant that makes managing money less of a chore and more like a conversation with a savvy friend who knows all about budgets and savings. It's especially handy for those just starting to engage with money independently, such as students and young adults fresh out of high school.

Meanwhile, Breathhh offers a different kind of assistance. It taps into the power of AI to guide you through mindfulness exercises. This is a machine learning-powered meditation coach available at the press of a button, helping you find your zen no matter where you are or how hectic your day gets.

For those who dread putting together presentations, Decktopus can step in to save the day. This AI-powered tool helps you whip up professional-looking slides in minutes, suggesting designs and content so you can focus on delivering your message without sweating over the aesthetics.

Then there's Lumen5, a dream come true for anyone who wishes to turn text into engaging video content. Let's say you're a blogger who wants to try your hand at video marketing or a small business owner looking to spruce up your online presence. Lumen5 makes this simple without requiring you to spend an extended amount of time learning yet another new tool. You provide the text and it helps you create a dynamic video, suggesting visuals and layouts that make your content pop.

If you want to get a little more "close and personal" with text-based AI without getting too technical, Replika offers a unique twist. It's an AI companion that learns from your conversations. This chatbot has been using true generative AI even before the legendary ChatGPT was around, which is quite a feat when you consider ChatGPT's monumental impact. Whether you need to vent, seek advice, or just share a moment of your day, Replika is there to listen and respond. When you talk to it, it might feel like you're interacting with a friend who is always there for you. But, as with every other lifelike chatbot, just be careful not to get too carried away. No matter how genuine it may seem, it's still a bot.

For hobbyists, there are some cool, user-friendly AI tools out there. If you love gardening, the Plantix app, a gardening expert in your pocket, can diagnose plant diseases from photos and suggest treatments.

Music lovers and those who enjoy relaxing with smooth tunes should try Endel, which creates personalized soundscapes to help you focus, relax, or sleep. The "artificial intelligence" aspect comes from the fact it uses data like your heart rate and the weather to tailor the sound for maximum positive vibes.

And for the artists or anyone who needs some extra creative inspiration, there's DeepArt, an AI that turns your photos into works of art in the styles of famous painters like Van Gogh or Picasso. All you have to do is upload a picture, choose your preferred style, and watch as it transforms your image into a masterpiece.

Photographers might like Luminar AI, which enhances your photos automatically. It suggests improvements and allows for quick edits that will make your pictures look professional with minimal effort and very little knowledge of video editing.

Lastly, imagine you need a photo's background gone—whether for a professional presentation or a fun personal project. Remove.bg is just one of the AI-powered tools that handles this task effortlessly and in mere seconds. It lets you focus on the creative part without getting bogged down by the technicalities of photo editing.

LEARNING AI BASICS

Artificial Intelligence (AI) might sound like something out of a sci-fi novel, but it's really not just for tech wizards or robot enthusiasts. If you're curious about how AI is reshaping industries or want to understand the hype around it, there are some fantastic resources out there that can help you achieve that—no tech background necessary.

First, check out AI for Non-Technical People: A Hands-On Beginner's Course, available on Udemy. This course breaks down AI into bite-sized, understandable pieces. It covers everything from the basics of AI to its application across different sectors like healthcare and finance. Plus, it wraps up with some neat projects you can do yourself without expensive equipment or advanced coding knowledge, allowing you to turn theory into practice.

Then there's Introduction to Artificial Intelligence by IBM on Coursera. This course is a tour through AI in its current form, explaining both the "what" and the "how" of AI applications. You'll get to explore various AI technologies, including how they're developed and the ethical issues they stir up. The best part is that it's structured in digestible segments that build on one another, so it's a guarantee that you won't be overwhelmed.

For those who want a broader view, AI for Everyone by Andrew Ng on Coursera is perfect. Led by one of the big names in AI, this course teaches the basics of AI and contextualizes it in the modern world. You'll learn about the impact of AI on society and jobs and pick up some insights on how to make it a part of your life.

For some elegant, slightly more traditional learning, consider Elements of AI from the University of Helsinki. This free online course has gained worldwide attention for its intent to make AI more accessible. What's fantastic about this course is its broad appeal. It targets everyone from students to professionals keen on understanding AI's societal impacts. You won't get held back by technical details here. Instead, you'll explore how AI is intertwined with real-life scenarios, making it incredibly relevant to daily discussions about technology.

Next up, Google's AI Education platform offers plenty of useful learning materials that cater to various levels of expertise. Its fundamentals section is particularly welcoming for newbies. This platform includes articles, videos, and a range of tutorials that teach the basics of AI and machine learning and guide you through implementing what you learn using Google's tools and resources. It's a hands-on way to see AI in action, from creating simple machine learning models to understanding data and neural networks.

And if you're someone who loves to learn in a more structured way, MIT's AI: Implications for Business Strategy is available through their Sloan School of Management in collaboration with GetSmarter. It's mainly for managers and business leaders, but this course outlines the strategic implications of AI in the business world, which may be exactly what you need. While it's a bit more niche, it's perfect if you're curious about how AI can transform industries and create new opportunities in the corporate world.

If you're looking for a more guided way to discover AI, Microsoft Learn could be just what you need. Microsoft Learn is like a travel guide that introduces you to landmarks (a.k.a. AI concepts) and then invites you to explore them through interactive activities. With Microsoft Learn, you get to try your hand at real AI tools directly on their Azure platform safely and completely without repercussions.

Now, if you're up for a class that combines a little celebrity with insights aplenty, Stanford University's Machine Learning course on Coursera is for you. The star of this course is also Andrew Ng, one of AI's big names, and he explains machine learning in a way that doesn't require a PhD or even particularly substantial computer science knowledge to understand. This course is full of short videos that break down complex topics into something digestible, and it's sprinkled with practical exercises that apply to real-world problems. The course is equally informative and genuinely useful.

For those who like to learn with a bit of elbow-rubbing with peers, Kaggle offers a brilliant world of ideas and challenges. You will jump directly into the fray when taking this hands-on course. You can pick from simple exercises to get started without much drama or take it further with competitions that pit your new skills against those of other learners. Everyone is there to figure out puzzles together, which means there is both camaraderie and a bit of friendly rivalry.

If you're interested in learning about AI by tinkering with tools, there are some great interactive platforms. For example, Google's Teachable Machine lets you train simple machine learning models online. It's a fun way to get hands-on experience with AI and is accessible to several age groups.

Podcasts, YouTube videos, and the like can also be a great way to learn. Shows like AI Alignment or Talking Machines feature experts discussing the latest in AI. They're perfect for staying informed while you're on the go.

You might also consider subscribing to AI newsletters to keep up with all the changes and new developments. After all, the field of AI changes practically every day. Import AI and The Algorithm from MIT Technology Review curate AI news and articles so you can stay in the loop without spending hours searching for information.

SETTING EXPECTATIONS

As you're learning about everything AI can do, it's easy to feel like you're walking into a time capsule taking you to the future. AI can seem like magic, like it can do anything, even better than humans. But in truth, it's more of a smart helper here to make lives easier within reason and limitations. So, let's set the record straight on what AI can (and can't) do, making sure you keep expectations firmly on the ground.

First, AI is fantastic at handling tasks that involve data processing, pattern recognition, and decision-making based on set parameters. For example, AI can analyze medical images with precision, manage your calendar by learning your schedule preferences, or drive your car (under certain conditions). It's an assistant who never sleeps and always remembers every tiny detail. But AI has already moved beyond repetitive tasks and can now generate new content. It can write, rewrite, or proofread articles, compose or remix music, or create art, which is pretty neat when you think about how it can support creative professionals.

However, AI isn't an all-knowing oracle. It works within the scope of the data it has been trained on, which means it can make mistakes, especially when it encounters a situation it hasn't seen before. Furthermore, since it doesn't have conscious awareness or knowledge of the outside world, it can make wild assumptions or "hallucinate", all in an attempt to fulfill a prompt. For example, AI might be great at identifying objects in photos under usual circumstances, but if you show it something totally out of context, it might get confused and make up the answer. This is because AI lacks general knowledge about the world—it doesn't understand context the way humans do.

Moreover, AI isn't great at understanding emotions or handling nuanced human interactions. It can try to do so, sometimes with a solid success rate, and it may give an incredibly emotionally intelligent response. Still, while there are chatbots that can mimic human conversation, they're not quite ready to replace human therapists or provide deep, meaningful advice on life's big questions. They work based on algorithms that match patterns in data, so their "understanding" is really just a reflection of what they've been programmed to recognize.

Another benefit of AI is that it can work incredibly quickly—much quicker than a human can. This is especially useful in fields like finance, where AI can analyze market data to provide investment insights or detect fraudulent transactions much faster than a human could. In healthcare, AI algorithms sift through vast amounts of medical data to predict patient outcomes, tailor treatments, or discover potential new drugs.

But here's where things get a bit sticky—AI is only as good as the data it's trained on. If the data is biased, incomplete, or worse, incorrect, the AI's decisions will be too. This is a significant limitation because it can lead to unfair, biased, or incorrect outcomes. For example, facial recognition systems have been known to fail to accurately identify people from certain backgrounds. Therefore, while AI is incredibly efficient, it requires careful oversight and diligent checks for fairness and accuracy.

Furthermore, AI doesn't possess true common sense or emotional intelligence, although it may do well at mimicking it. It can't make moral decisions or understand ethical nuances the way humans can. This means that in situations requiring ethical judgment, like law enforcement or social services, AI can support human decision-makers but not replace them. It lacks the ability to understand complex human emotions and societal contexts, which are often the deciding factors in these fields. It's for a good reason that in popular culture, leaving all the societal decisions to an AI is portrayed as poor judgment. It's because, in truth, it is.

And while AI can automate many tasks, there are creative and interpersonal aspects of jobs that AI simply can't replicate. For example, while AI can assist in composing music or drafting articles, it doesn't truly "create" in the human sense. It doesn't experience inspiration or intuition but rather creates in a purely mechanical, formally logical manner. Therefore, only humans can come up with wholly new ideas and concepts or create expressive, genuinely emotional art. Similarly, in roles that require deep personal interactions like teaching, nursing, or counseling, AI can provide tools and support but cannot replace the human connection that is central to these professions.

To keep things real, let's talk about the rules and guidelines around AI. As AI gets more advanced, there are ongoing efforts to create regulations for its responsible use. The European Union is working on an AI Act, and there are guidelines from organizations like the IEEE that set rules to make AI systems safe and transparent and ensure they respect privacy. While these efforts do address ethical concerns, in some ways, they may make AI more limited. This means if you're using an AI app in Europe, it's likely meeting some pretty strict standards. Depending on how the regulations are applied or interpreted, some (unintentional or otherwise) creative restrictions and constraints may arise. It may take a few rewrites and attempts before there can be a balance between ethical regulation and freedom of expression and creativity.

In the U.S., there isn't a single AI law yet, but states like California are leading the way with laws like the California Consumer Privacy Act (CCPA). This law impacts how AI can collect and use personal data. It aims to protect consumers but also makes it a bit tougher for companies to roll out new AI tech quickly.

Companies are also trying to align with these regulations. For instance, Google has set its own AI principles, focusing on things like avoiding bias and ensuring AI is used for good. It is meant to follow the rules and build trust with users who might be wary of how their data is being used.

While these regulations are necessary for creating AI that benefits everyone and doesn't cause more problems, they also mean developers have to be extra careful. This can slow down the rollout of new technologies, but it also helps make sure everything is done right, which is better in the long run.

So, what's the main takeaway regarding setting your expectations about AI? All these considerations and limitations show that AI works best when paired with human expertise. For example, in healthcare, AI can analyze data, but doctors make the final decisions about treatment. The teamwork between AI and humans leads to better results and is safer and more reasonable than relying on a tool that doesn't truly "get" the world around it.

CHAPTER 8

DIY GUIDES TO IMPLEMENTING AI AT HOME

Getting hands-on with AI doesn't require a PhD in computer science. With some time, basic (or slightly more advanced) tools, and a bit of curiosity, you can start creating your own AI projects at home. This chapter will guide you through some simple and practical exercises to help you get started with AI.

Think of it as a fun weekend project that teaches you something new and makes your life a bit easier or more interesting. AI can assist you in a number of ways. You could set up a smart home device, build a simple chatbot, or experiment with AI in your favorite video game. There's something here for everyone at almost any skill level, interest, or age. You don't need to be a tech expert to get started. However, what you do need is a willingness to learn and a little bit of patience.

By the end of this chapter, you'll have a few cool AI tricks up your sleeve and a better understanding of how AI works in everyday applications. It's easier than you might think and fun, too.

PRACTICAL EXERCISES

You never have to miss an important email or notification again. Setting up an automated alert system is a straightforward project that introduces you to AI without overwhelming you. Start by signing up for a free account on a platform like Zapier or IFTTT. These platforms let you create automated workflows that are called "zaps" or "applets". These "applets" and "zaps" connect your favorite apps and services. For example, you can set up a workflow that sends a notification to your phone every time you receive an email from a specific contact or with a particular keyword. This way, you'll always be on top of your most important communications without constantly checking your inbox.

Another fun project is building a basic chatbot. Chatbots are a great way to see AI in action and can be surprisingly simple to create. Begin by using a platform like Chatfuel or BotStar, which offers user-friendly interfaces for building chatbots without any coding. You can design your chatbot to answer frequently asked questions, share information about a hobby, or just chat for fun. The first thing to do is to define the purpose of your chatbot and then create a series of responses based on common questions or prompts. As you get more comfortable, you can add more complex features. You could integrate the chatbot with other services or use natural language processing to make the chatbot's responses more sophisticated and more realistic.

Building your own AI model might sound intimidating. If you're too ambitious and don't have the right skills, it can be. But simpler AI models can be quite manageable with the right tools. Platforms like Google's Teachable Machine let you train a simple machine learning model in your web browser. You can create a model that recognizes images, sounds, or poses and use it for fun projects like a custom gesture-based controller for your computer. Training these custom models involves uploading examples of what you want the AI to recognize, letting it learn from these examples, and then testing the model to see how well it performs. It's a hands-on way to understand the basics of machine learning and see the results in real-time. Once done, it can be quite practical, too.

You can also explore AI in home automation with platforms like Home Assistant or SmartThings. These tools let you automate your home devices and make daily life a bit easier. Imagine coming home and your lights turning on by themselves or your thermostat adjusting to the perfect temperature. To get started, you just need to connect your smart devices to the platform using your phone. Once everything is set up, you create rules that fit your routine, like having your lights turn on when you arrive home, or your coffee maker start brewing when you wake up. You can even get creative and set up more complex automation, like having your smart speakers play your favorite playlist as soon as you walk in the door or your blinds adjust based on the time of day. It's cool to see how much convenience AI can bring into your daily routine without requiring incredibly expensive "futuristic" tools.

Voice assistants like Alexa and Google Assistant are another fun way to use AI at home. Beyond the basics, like playing music or setting reminders, you can create custom routines that link multiple actions together. As an example, you could set a morning routine where one command triggers a series of actions. For example, the phrase 'Good morning" could trigger your AI assistant to begin reading you the news, start your coffee maker, give you a weather update, and turn on your smart lights. It's like having a mini butler to help you kickstart the day. This saves you time and shows off what AI can really do. You can also link your assistant with other smart home devices to create a system that works perfectly for you. Maybe you want an evening routine that turns off all the lights, locks the doors, and sets the thermostat to your favorite sleeping temperature. Experimenting with these routines can be a lot of fun and another great way to see how AI can seamlessly fit into your life, making it more convenient and efficient.

If you're interested in data science, Jupyter Notebooks with Python libraries like Pandas and Scikit-learn is a fantastic place to start. These tools let you analyze data sets and build simple models, giving you a hands-on intro to AI and data science. Start with free data sets from places like Kaggle. You can practice cleaning the data, exploring it, and making predictions. For instance, you could use a data set to predict housing prices, analyze trends in stock markets, or look at patterns in social media. This isn't just about playing with numbers, although that is certainly the fun part for some. But it also lets you see how AI can be used to solve real-world problems. Working through these projects helps you understand how AI and data science intersect and gives you valuable skills you can use in various fields. Plus, there's a satisfying sense of achievement when your predictions start to make sense, and you see the practical applications of what you're learning.

If you're into gaming, creating a simple AI for a game can be quite enjoyable, too. Game engines like Unity have awesome tutorials that guide you through adding AI to game characters. You can program them to move and react in specific ways, which makes the game much more engaging. Imagine creating characters that follow the player, avoid obstacles, or interact with other characters in interesting ways.

Now, keep in mind that in gaming, "AI" has a bit of a double meaning. On the one hand, it has been used since the early days to refer to any behavior of non-player characters (NPCs), including the most basic actions. Traditional AI in games doesn't mean software harnessing machine learning or neural networks. However, it can cover everything from simple enemy sprites moving about the screen and trying to "get" the player to complex characters with varying routines, reactions, skills, character progressions, and more. On the other hand, we have AI that does employ new technologies, like neural networks. The two definitions are a perfect match for each other and can converge, so why not try your hand at both?

For example, you could start with a basic enemy character that chases the player when they get too close. You'd use basic video game AI concepts like pathfinding, which helps your character get around the game environment. As you get more comfortable, you can add complexity, like making the enemies smarter over time so that they learn from the player's movements or work together to create a more challenging gameplay.

You could also create friendly NPCs that provide help or add depth to your game world. Maybe you program a shopkeeper who sells items and offers advice based on what the player has done in the game. Or perhaps you design a companion character that follows the player, helps in battles, and reacts to the player's actions and decisions throughout the game.

Working on AI in games lets you mix creativity with technical skills. You get to design characters that feel alive and responsive, making the game world more immersive. It's really satisfying to see your AI-driven characters come to life, interacting with players in ways that make the game feel immersive and believable.

Adding AI to your games also opens up endless possibilities for gameplay mechanics. You can create puzzles where players have to outsmart AI opponents or develop complex ecosystems where AI-driven animals behave in realistic ways. The more you experiment, the more you'll see how AI can turn simple game concepts into rich, interactive experiences.

Plus, as you get deeper into game AI, you'll learn about more advanced techniques like machine learning, which create even more sophisticated behaviors. Introducing machine learning can make AI that adapts to the player's playstyle for a different challenge each time they play. Or think about using procedural generation techniques to create endless game worlds based on AI algorithms, as displayed in games such as No Man's Sky.

BUILDING YOUR OWN AI MODEL

Once you've mastered the basics of building AI models with Teachable Machine and similar above-mentioned tools and feel confident enough in your skills, you can give more advanced projects a go. For example, you can use platforms such as TensorFlow and Google Colab to build more complex models. Google Colab runs comfortably on the cloud and lets you write and run Python code without installing special Integrated Development Environments (IDEs) locally. It is great for working with AI, even if you don't have a system powerful enough to comfortably run more advanced AI models. Meanwhile, TensorFlow is a powerful open-source library for machine learning that lets you build and train models for various tasks. It runs locally, so you aren't bound by the Internet or any other restrictions that come with cloud-based tools. You can start by following tutorials to get a feel for how TensorFlow works and then move on to creating your own models.

You can also do your own sentiment analysis. For example, collect a dataset of tweets or Facebook comments, then use pre-processing techniques to clean the text data and train a TensorFlow model to classify the sentiment as positive, negative, or neutral. Google Colab is perfect for this because it provides the computing power you need without the hassle of setting up your own environment. Once trained, you can test your model by feeding it new social media posts and seeing how accurately it predicts the sentiment.

Another exciting project is using AI to personalize recommendations. You could build a recommendation system similar to Netflix or Amazon's. First, you will need to gather data on your preferences—this could be movies you like, books you've read, or products you frequently buy. Using this data, you can train a model to suggest new items that match your tastes. This involves understanding algorithms like collaborative filtering and content-based filtering, which might be slightly more advanced. However, they are commonly used in recommendation systems, so finding information on them isn't difficult.

With TensorFlow, you can create a chatbot that understands context and provides more relevant responses. Begin by collecting a dataset of conversations relevant to your chatbot's purpose. Preprocess this data and use it to train a neural network model. Incorporate natural language processing (NLP) techniques to enhance the chatbot's ability to understand and generate human-like responses. Google Colab's collaborative environment allows you to share your progress and get feedback in real-time, making the development process smoother and more interactive. Once your chatbot is trained, you could integrate it with platforms like Slack or your website for real-world testing and use.

If you enjoy working with images, you might want to explore image classification and object detection. With tools like OpenCV and, once again, TensorFlow, you can create models that identify objects in images or detect faces. For example, you could build a model that scans photos and identifies different types of plants or animals. For this project, you'll need to collect a sizeable dataset of images, label them, and train your model to recognize the patterns. This is a great way to see how AI can be used in fields like biology or environmental science, beyond simple online image tagging.

Voice recognition is another fascinating area to explore. You can use platforms like Mozilla's DeepSpeech or Google's Speech-to-Text

API to create models that understand and process human speech. This could be useful if you want to build a virtual assistant that responds to voice commands or transcribes spoken words into text. Start by recording various voice samples and then train your model to recognize and interpret them. Giving this project a go can give you a deeper understanding of how natural language processing and voice-activated systems work.

If you're into numbers and data, creating predictive models is both challenging and rewarding. Perhaps you could use AI to predict stock market trends or forecast weather patterns. This involves gathering historical data, cleaning and preprocessing it, and then training a model to make accurate predictions based on past trends. Tools like Scikit-learn and TensorFlow make it easier to build these types of models, and there are plenty of online resources to help you, so it isn't as difficult and technical as it may appear at first. However, it is still a more advanced project.

Lastly, you might consider experimenting with generative models like Generative Adversarial Networks (GANs) to create new content. This may be the most advanced of the projects mentioned, but it is very rewarding. GANs consist of two neural networks—the generator and the discriminator—that work together to produce realistic data. You can use GANs to generate text, images, music, and perhaps even short video clips. Yes, the project is more advanced, but it can be quite fun once you get the hang of it and has the potential to really show the creative value of AI. There are numerous tutorials available online that can help you get started with building and training your own GANs.

MORE ON AI ART AND MUSIC

Making AI art and music is a fantastic way to see the creative (and slightly controversial) side of artificial intelligence. You don't have to be a professional artist to get started, although knowing a bit about art techniques, music genres, art and music theory, and so on can certainly help.

For art, there are platforms like DeepArt and DeepDream. These tools use AI to turn your photos into artwork in the style of famous painters like Van Gogh or Picasso. All you need to do is upload a photo, choose an art style, and let the AI work its magic. It's fascinating to see how your everyday snapshots can become something that looks like it belongs in a gallery, and it happens in a matter of seconds. Of course, it won't put you on the list of top artists in history since it's only doing a re-touch, but the effect is captivating anyway.

If you're into music, tools like Amper Music, Udio, Suno, and Jukedeck help you create original compositions. These platforms let you pick the genre, mood, and instruments, and the AI generates a unique piece of music for you. You can use these compositions as background music for videos, podcasts, or just for fun. The AI takes your input and produces a complete song in minutes. Some of these tools let you generate lyrics and write your own, and then an AI voice can sign the song in the correct style. It even gets the language and accent right.

Another exciting artistic way to use AI is to collaborate on creative projects with it. Maybe you could start a painting and let an AI finish it, or you could create a melody and see how an AI develops it into a full song. You could even give it a rough first draft for a story and let it help you flesh it out and point out any plotholes or areas for improvement. This kind of collaboration can lead to surprising and inspiring results. It helps people who enjoy creative pursuits but could use a little extra push from time to time.

There are also apps like Magenta from Google that let you go deeper into AI-generated art and music. Magenta has tools and tutorials for creating AI-powered art and music projects that give you more control and allow for more complex creations.

AI FOR IMAGE AND VIDEO RECOGNITION

If you can use AI to make visual art and music, why not try having it recognize things within images and videos? This step is a bit more involved, but you will love the results.

First, let's talk about images. There are platforms like Google's Teachable Machine that make it really easy to train an AI model to recognize different objects in a picture, even when the image may be hazy or have artifacts. All you need to do is gather some images of the objects you want the AI to recognize. For example, if you want your AI to tell the difference between cats and dogs, take or find a bunch of pictures of each. Upload these images to the Teachable Machine, label them, and let the AI start learning. In just a few minutes, you'll have a model that can look at a new image and tell you if it's a cat or a dog. Having your model recognize things correctly after your training is very satisfying.

Video recognition is just as exciting, if a little more involved. You can use tools like OpenCV and TensorFlow to train models that analyze video frames frame-by-frame. For example, you can create a system that monitors a camera feed and recognizes specific actions or movements. You could set up a camera in your garden and train the AI to spot when birds visit your bird feeder. You can do this by recording videos of birds and other common garden visitors and then feeding these videos into your model for training. Before you know it, you'll have an AI that can alert you whenever a bird stops by. Or, if you're more concerned by security, teach the AI to tell your usual activities from suspicious happenings that your security camera catches. It's not as adorable as birdwatching, but it can surely be practical.

Another fun project is building a facial recognition system. Using a Raspberry Pi and a camera, you can train an AI to recognize the faces of your family and friends. You'd do this by first taking pictures of the people you want the AI to recognize. Then, upload these to your training platform (with permission from the person in the photo, of course), label each face, and let the AI learn. Once trained, set up the camera at your door, and your AI can greet people by name or unlock the door for familiar faces. This AI is your own personal doorman who never takes a break.

Also, if you love a bit of extra challenge, try training an AI to recognize emotions from facial expressions. You can use datasets that include images of different facial expressions labeled with emotions like happiness, sadness, anger, and surprise. Training the AI on these images helps it learn to interpret human emotions, which could be useful in applications like virtual assistants or customer service bots.

AUTONOMOUS ROBOTICS WITH AI

What exactly are autonomous robots? As the name hints, autonomous robots are robots that perform tasks without constant human supervision. Unsurprisingly, it's thanks to AI that these bots can function so effectively on their own. They learn from their environment and make their own decisions using AI technology. A great way to explore this field is with a robot kit like those from LEGO Mindstorms or VEX Robotics. These kits come with all the parts you need to build your robot and include easy-to-follow instructions. Once you've built the robot, you can program it to perform simple tasks, like solving a maze or avoiding obstacles.

If you have some basic knowledge of electronics (and perhaps the ability to solder), Arduino and Raspberry Pi are perfect for beginners and hobbyists. Arduino is great for controlling simple robotic components like motors and sensors. Raspberry Pi, on the other hand, is a small computer that has the power to run more complex AI algorithms. You can use these systems to write simple code to program a robot to move around or use sensors to detect and avoid obstacles. Luckily, these platforms are quite popular among electronics enthusiasts, meaning there are tons of tutorials online to get started.

Once you get more comfortable, you can then integrate AI to make your robot smarter. For example, try using computer vision to help your robot see and understand its surroundings. OpenCV and similar tools can process images from a camera mounted on your robot and help it recognize objects. You can teach your robot to identify and pick up objects or follow specific colors. It's like giving your robot a pair of eyes.

Another nifty project to try is using machine learning to improve the bot's performance over time. Imagine building a robot that can navigate a path and learn from its mistakes. You can use reinforcement learning, a type of machine learning, to create a robot that gets better at tasks by receiving feedback. Every time the robot completes a task correctly, it gets a reward. If it fails, it gets a penalty. Over time, the robot learns to make better decisions and perform the task more efficiently.

Building a robotic arm that can sort objects is a fantastic hands-on AI project. Start with a robotics kit, assemble your robotic arm, and attach a camera. Use OpenCV to help your robot recognize different objects. Train a simple machine learning model to classify objects by color, shape, or size using labeled images. Connect your model to the robotic arm's control system so it knows how to sort the objects based on the classification. As always, the Internet has practically everything you need in terms of resources. There are plenty of online tutorials and communities where you can get help and inspiration if you get stuck.

If you're up for more of a challenge, try building a self-navigating car. Begin with a small, off-the-shelf robot car kit. Install a Raspberry Pi and a camera to serve as the car's eyes. Use TensorFlow to train an object detection model that helps the car recognize and avoid obstacles. You'll need to gather training data by driving the car manually and recording the camera feed along with the steering commands. Once you finish training your model, upload it to the Raspberry Pi and connect it to the car's control system. Open-source libraries like Donkey Car can make this all much simpler, giving you a framework for the car's software and AI components.

One of the most fun aspects of autonomous robotics is experimenting with different sensors and actuators. You can add ultrasonic sensors for obstacle detection, infrared sensors for line following, or GPS modules if you want the bot to find its way outside, even over longer distances. Combining these sensors with AI makes your robot incredibly versatile. You could build a robot that maps out a room, detects changes in its environment, and adjusts its path accordingly.

If you want to take things to the next level, try building a drone. Drones are essentially flying robots and can be programmed to perform autonomous flights. You can use AI to help the drone avoid obstacles, follow moving objects, or perform aerial photography missions, so if you like taking sweeping images or videos, it's perfect. Of course, this is a bit more advanced, but the skills you learn from ground-based robots translate nicely to drones.

CHATBOTS FOR SOCIAL MEDIA

There seems to be quite a close association between artificial intelligence and chatbots. It's hardly a surprise. After all, what better way to experience artificial intelligence first-hand than to talk to something that can talk back? Not only do chatbots talk back, but nowadays, they can do it in a way that feels natural and very close to how a real person would speak.

First things first, to build a chatbot for social media, you'll need a platform to build that chatbot. Chatfuel and ManyChat are both user-friendly and perfect for beginners. These platforms have a convenient drag-and-drop interface, so you don't need to write code yourself. Sign up for a free account and pick the social media platform where you want your chatbot to live. Facebook Messenger is popular, but you can also create bots for Instagram, WhatsApp, Discord, and other platforms.

Next, think about what you want the chatbot to do. Is it going to provide customer service, share information about a topic, or just have fun conversations? Once you have a goal in mind, you can design the flow of the conversation. For example, if you're building a customer service bot, you might set it up to answer common questions about store hours, return policies, or product details. You can create different paths in the conversation flow based on user responses, making the interaction feel like it's happening between two real humans.

One of the cool features you can add to your chatbot is the ability to handle more complex interactions using natural language processing. Dialogflow and Wit.ai can help your bot understand and respond to user input more naturally. For instance, if someone types a question in their own words, NLP can help the bot interpret the meaning and provide a relevant response. NLP makes the conversation feel more human-like and less scripted.

As you build your chatbot, don't forget to add some personality. Give your bot a name, and write responses that match the tone you want. If your bot is supposed to be fun and casual, keep the language light and friendly. If it's for something more formal, like doing business, make the responses professional and helpful but still relatable enough that it doesn't put users off.

Once your chatbot is ready, it's time to test it out. Share it with friends or colleagues and ask for feedback before you make it public. Sharing with a smaller group will help you spot issues and refine the bot's responses. You must test the bot before deploying it because it helps you understand how real users will interact with your bot.

After testing, you can integrate your chatbot with your social media accounts. How exactly you do this varies depending on the platform, but it usually involves linking your bot to your social media page and creating some basic settings. Once integrated, your chatbot will be live and ready to interact with your audience.

Keep in mind that building a chatbot is not a one-and-done activity. Monitor its interactions, gather data on how users are engaging with it, and make improvements over time. The more you tweak and refine your bot, the better it will perform.

Once your chatbot is up and running, you can use analytics tools like Chatbase or Botanalytics to measure user engagement and track how users interact with your bot. These tools let you see which parts of the conversation flow smoothly and where users tend to drop off or get confused. By analyzing this data, you can spot patterns and identify areas where your chatbot might need improvement. Then, you can train it a bit more and try again.

For example, if you notice that many users are asking the same question that your bot isn't prepared to answer, you can update the bot's responses to include that information. If users often abandon the conversation at a specific point, it could be a sign that the instructions or options are unclear. Adjust the flow or language to make things smoother. Regularly reviewing your chatbot's performance data helps you fine-tune its interactions, making the experience better for users and more effective for achieving your goals. It's a continuous process of learning and tweaking, just like training the bot itself.

CHAPTER 9

PREPARING FOR AN AI-POWERED FUTURE

So far, this guide has explored a lot about AI—its applications, benefits, and some hands-on projects you can try at home without being a tech whiz. But there's more to the story. AI isn't just about understanding the technology and using it as it is at the moment. Much more than that, it's also about thinking ahead and preparing for the future because, no matter where the future takes it, artificial intelligence is here to stay and will only get more advanced.

In this chapter, we're going to take a look at some forward-thinking topics that might help you stay ahead of the curve. Among other topics, we'll talk about the significance of lifelong learning in the ever-changing, never-resting field of AI, how to introduce AI concepts to kids, and the role of AI in promoting sustainable living. The chapter will also take a peek into the future, imagining how AI might continue to change the world in exciting, unexpected, and, at times, unsettling ways.

LIFELONG LEARNING

One of the best ways to keep learning about AI is by taking online courses. Websites like Coursera, Udemy, and Khan Academy offer AI courses at beginner, intermediate, and expert levels. Some of the courses have been mentioned in earlier chapters, but new courses keep popping up, so it's worth keeping an eye out for content that meets your needs. You can find courses that teach you the basics, like what AI is and how it works, as well as more advanced topics like machine learning and neural networks. The great thing about these courses is that you can learn at your own pace. If you're busy, you can watch a short video here and there, and if you have more time, you can go deep into the material.

Reading books is yet another great way to learn and keep up. There are plenty of books out there that explain AI in a way that's easy to understand, even if you don't have a technical background. Some popular titles include AI Superpowers by Kai-Fu Lee and Life 3.0 by Max Tegmark. These books give you a broad overview of AI and its potential impact on the future, and they're pretty engaging reads.

Don't underestimate the power of podcasts and YouTube channels, either. There are some fantastic podcasts like AI Alignment and Talking Machines that feature experts discussing the latest in AI. You can listen to these while you're commuting, working out, or doing chores. Similarly, YouTube channels like Two Minute Papers break down complex AI topics into bite-sized videos that are easy to digest. Plus, they often show the latest research and developments in the field.

Joining a local or online AI community can also be really beneficial if you live somewhere that makes it possible. These communities host meetups, workshops, and discussions where you can learn from others and share your own insights. Websites like Meetup.com might help you find AI groups in your area, while Reddit and Discord have active AI communities where you can ask questions and join conversations. It just takes a bit of time to discover and decide what to join.

There are also some awesome resources to get kids and teens interested in AI early on. Places like Scratch, for example, have excellent programming courses for young learners, and there are even AI kits available that let kids build their own simple AI projects. Some Arduino kits are also meant for younger enthusiasts to try building electronics and "smart" devices. Introducing children to AI concepts early might spark their curiosity and help them adapt better to whatever new technology comes up in the future.

One fun way to keep learning about AI is by playing around with AI tools and apps. One app we've discussed already, Replika, lets you chat with an AI bot, which can be both entertaining and educational because you gradually learn how a bot responds to you versus how a person might. A chatbot like Claude or ChatGPT may do the same, and each has a different style, capabilities, and limitations. Therefore, having even merely casual conversations with these bots can keep you in the AI loop and help you recognize patterns. By exploring these bots, you get to see firsthand how AI handles conversations and even develops a personality over time based on your interactions. You will experience AI in a more personal, hands-on manner and may even pick up on a few AI-isms (common words and phrases that a certain model loves to use). It turns out that just as we all have some go-to words and phrases, so does AI.

Another idea is to follow AI influencers and experts on social media. They may present new developments in a fun and easy-to-follow way. Many knowledgeable people use Twitter and LinkedIn regularly to share insights, news, and cool projects. Following these experts can keep you in the loop with the latest trends and discoveries in AI, and you might even find some inspiration for your own projects.

Workshops and seminars are also great ways to continuously and seamlessly learn more about AI topics. Many universities and tech companies offer free or low-cost workshops, sometimes virtually, other times in person. These can range from beginner-level introductions to more advanced, specialized topics. Attending a workshop is fantastic if you wish to get hands-on experience, ask questions, and meet others who share your interest in AI.

If you prefer something with a bit more structure, you might consider enrolling in a certification program. Universities and online platforms have certification courses in AI and machine learning. These programs cover a wide range of topics and provide a more in-depth understanding on an academic level. Plus, having a certification can be a nice boost to your resume if you want to incorporate AI skills into your career. Most of the time, more certificates are better than fewer.

If you love a good challenge, participating in AI competitions can be an exciting way to learn. Competitions give you opportunities to keep learning and constantly testing your skills. They also give you a taste of how to apply your AI skills to solve real-world problems. These competitions often come with datasets and specific goals, pushing you to think creatively and apply what you've learned in a competitive setting. You get to test your skills, learn new techniques, and win prizes or recognition. Being competitive is perhaps one of the best ways to continue learning and improving.

Also, don't forget to share what you learn with others. Teaching and talking about your achievements and failures reinforces what you've learned. Write a blog post about a cool AI project you've done, make a YouTube tutorial, or just chat with friends and family. Sharing your knowledge helps solidify what you've learned in your own head and might inspire others to learn about AI for themselves.

TEACHING CHILDREN

Children are naturally curious and love to explore new things, so teaching them about AI can tap into that sense of wonder and excitement. Besides, it helps prepare them for a future where technology will play an even bigger role and where AI is here to stay.

One of the best ways to start is by using educational tools and toys that teach coding and AI basics. Scratch uses a simple, visual programming language that lets kids create their own interactive stories, games, and animations. They can learn the logic behind coding without getting bogged down by complex syntax. It playfully introduces the building blocks of AI and coding in general. Better yet, it won't feel like they're learning something overly technical or mathematical, both of which are sometimes offputting to children. With this interactive format, they will gain these skills subtly, and before they know it, they'll be able to tackle more advanced tools in a heartbeat.

Robotics kits are another fantastic way to get kids interested in AI. Kits from LEGO Mindstorms or VEX Robotics come with all the parts necessary to build and program their own robots. Kids can learn how to make their robots move, avoid obstacles, or respond to voice commands. Kits from companies like Sphero and Ozobot are just as useful for teaching programming and AI concepts through play. These kits come with step-by-step instructions and lots of online resources that make it easy for kids to start learning.

There are also fun apps and games that teach programming and AI concepts in a more interactive way. For example, the app Swift Playgrounds teaches kids coding in Swift through engaging puzzles and challenges. As they progress, users start to understand how programming and, by extension, AI work. Another great app is Kodable, which introduces coding fundamentals in a game-like setting, which is perfect for younger children.

Unleashing the power of technology can be exhilarating for kids. Books and online resources can be super helpful. Take Hello Ruby: Adventures in Coding by Linda Liukas, for example. It's a great book that uses fun stories to teach kids about coding and computational thinking. On YouTube, there are awesome channels like Code.org that share plenty of tutorials and inspiring videos. These channels show real kids getting hands-on with technology, making it all seem less intimidating and more accessible.

Storytime is a great way to introduce AI concepts. Plenty of children's books explain AI in simple, engaging ways. You can read these books to children instead of the same old storybook you've read to them a dozen times. Books like My First Coding Book by Kiki Prottsman and A Kid's Guide to Artificial Intelligence (AI) by Amber Lovett make learning about AI fun and easy to understand.

Using virtual assistants like Alexa or Google Assistant can also be educational and fun. Show kids how these devices work and explain the basics of voice recognition. You can even create simple Alexa skills together using Amazon's Alexa Skills Kit.

Working on small AI projects with your children can be an engaging and interesting way for them to learn and for you to bond. You could start by building a simple chatbot using free online platforms. Let your child come up with the questions and responses, and then show them how the chatbot works. It's a hands-on activity that makes AI concepts easy to grasp and a lot of fun to play with.

Or, try making a basic sensor system together. Using inexpensive sensors and a simple microcontroller like an Arduino, kids can learn how sensors collect data and how AI uses this data to make decisions. Imagine creating a plant watering system that waters the plant when the soil is dry—this is a hands-on way to show your kid how AI can solve everyday problems.

Also, don't forget to highlight the creative side of AI. You've seen how you can use sites like DeepArt and tools like Amper Music. These sites are also a great way to allow kids to see how AI can be used to create art and music. They show the young ones that AI isn't just coding and programming, but also applies to creativity and imagination. They can make artwork straight from their dreams or compose their own music with a little help from AI.

Learning through group activities is awesome for many kids. Working with friends makes learning more fun and develops teamwork skills. Organize playdates or group projects where kids can collaborate on AI-related activities. They can work together to build a robot, create a simple AI game, or participate in AI competitions for kids.

Getting kids involved in tech clubs or coding camps is yet another fantastic idea, especially if they're on the more sociable side. Many schools and communities have clubs where kids can work on tech projects together. These clubs are awesome for learning, making friends, and collaborating on projects. Coding camps, whether in-person or online, are immersive, and kids can learn about all the exciting concepts in technology, including artificial intelligence.

When your kids start asking questions about their favorite video games or how a robot works, that's the perfect time to explain some basics. You don't need to get too technical. All you have to do is spark their curiosity by explaining how they can create these things themselves. It's all about showing them that they can be creators, not just users, of the technology they love.

Get them thinking about how AI can solve problems they care about or make something they've always wanted to do a reality. Ask them how they could use AI to keep their room tidy, help with their homework, make fanart of their favorite cartoon character, or create a cool new game. This kind of brainstorming leads to some pretty creative ideas and helps them see AI as a tool they can use.

It's also good to show them real-world examples of AI in action. Talk about how AI is used in things they already know, like recommendation systems on Netflix or Spotify, self-driving cars, or smart home devices. Understanding how AI impacts their world can make learning more relevant and exciting because they'll learn to recognize its presence when they see it.

Also, talk to kids about the ethical side of AI. Teaching them to consider the ethical implications of technology early on helps them become responsible tech users and creators once they're a little older. Talk to them about why it's important to think about data privacy and the impact of AI decisions.

AI IN SUSTAINABLE LIVING

There are a bunch of ways AI is making it easier for us to take care of the planet. Some might blame technology for many of the planet's ills, but the truth is that it goes both ways. Yes, technology has had some pretty unfortunate impacts on the planet, but at the same time, it is also making a real positive difference. AI is no exception. It helps improve people's lives in many areas, including urban, rural, and wild settings, and everything in between. While it is true that AI itself comes with some environmental concerns, especially given the monumental energy necessary for training and running large models, it can offset this by helping environmentalism in other ways. Once you know all the ways AI can help the environment, you can imagine how it can shape the future of conservation.

For starters, think about how you use energy at home. Smart thermostats like Nest use AI to learn your routine and adjust the temperature automatically. So, if you usually leave the house at 8 a.m., your thermostat will turn down the heating or cooling to save energy. This little helper makes sure your home is comfortable when you're there and saves energy when you're not. Over time, it learns your preferences, like if you prefer it cooler at night or warmer in the mornings, and adjusts accordingly without you having to lift a finger. It may seem like it prioritizes your comfort over being green, but in reality, it does both. Once the monthly utility bill arrives, you will see just how much more energy efficient these thermostats can be compared to the old-fashioned ones, given the right settings and patterns. It's pretty neat to see how much energy (and money) you can save just by letting the AI do its thing.

Smart lighting is another cool example. These systems use sensors and AI to adjust the lights depending on the time of day or whether someone's in the room. It's a simple change, but it makes a big difference in cutting down your electricity use without you even thinking about it. Your lights dim in the evening to help you wind down or turn off automatically when you leave a room. This means no more forgetting to turn off the lights and wasting electricity. You can even set them to mimic natural daylight patterns, which can be great for your mood and productivity.

AI is also making a big splash in waste management (not in the unhygienic way). There are AI-powered robots that sort through recycling much more efficiently than humans can. These robots use cameras and machine learning to tell different materials apart and sort them correctly. This means fewer items end up in the wrong bin, and more materials actually get recycled. Imagine a robot that can pick out plastic bottles from a pile of trash in the blink of an eye. It's kind of like having a super-fast, super-accurate helper that gives more items a second chance at life, reducing the amount of waste that ends up in landfills. Plus, it takes some of the guesswork out of recycling, which can be confusing at times.

In farming, AI is making a big impact by helping farmers use resources more wisely. AI-powered drones and sensors can monitor crop health, soil conditions, and weather. This info lets farmers water and fertilize their crops more precisely, reducing waste and boosting yields. It's like giving farmers a super high-tech toolkit to grow food more efficiently and sustainably. Imagine a drone flying over a field, taking detailed images, and using AI to analyze the health of the plants. The drone can spot problems, like pests or diseases, early and even suggest the best treatments. This means healthier crops and less wasted resources, which is a win-win for farmers and the environment.

Artificial intelligence in farming also predicts the best times to plant and harvest by analyzing weather patterns and historical data. AI can help farmers make decisions that will produce the best possible crop yields while wasting as few resources as reasonably possible, which is a great win for the environment. This kind of precision farming means less guesswork and more efficient use of land and resources. Plus, it can help farmers adapt to changing climates and keep their crops resilient, which is important considering increasingly changing and unpredictable climate events.

Water management is another area where AI does a good job at potentially making the world a little greener. Smart irrigation systems use AI to check weather forecasts and soil moisture levels to decide when and how much to water plants. This knowledge avoids overwatering and saves water, which is especially important in drought-prone areas. For example, people have designed AI-boosted gardens that water themselves just the right amount. These systems can also send alerts if there's a leak or if the soil needs extra attention to conserve water and for plants to get exactly what they need to thrive.

AI is also helping protect wildlife. Conservationists use AI to track endangered animals and monitor their habitats. AI-powered cameras spot poachers in wildlife reserves and alert rangers to take action. This tech is incredibly powerful in protecting endangered species and keeping ecosystems balanced. Conservation using AI involves hiding cameras in the habitats of endangered species and using AI to recognize and report suspicious activity in real-time. This allows rangers to respond quickly and stop illegal activities to save animals from harm.

Beyond protecting animals from poachers, AI can monitor animal populations and health. For example, AI can analyze images and videos to count animals and track their movements. This information helps conservationists understand how animals are using their habitats and how to protect them better. It's like having a team of biologists working around the clock, gathering data that can inform better conservation strategies. But unlike human biologists, AI never tires. Well-designed AI systems may also be less likely to make mistakes.

As you might know, AI is behind a lot of the advancements in electric and self-driving cars. Of course, it can control the driving itself, but on the side of environmentalism, there are some lesser-known benefits. AI makes electric cars more efficient by optimizing how well the car uses its battery. AI can analyze your driving habits and adjust how the car uses its battery to make sure you get the most out of each charge. This means you can drive longer distances without needing to recharge, which is super convenient, especially on long trips, and better yet, saves energy and the planet. AI can also predict when you'll need to recharge and guide you to the nearest charging station, taking the stress out of finding one on the fly.

Self-driving cars use AI to navigate and drive in a way that saves fuel and reduces emissions. These cars have a range of sensors and cameras that feed data to the AI system, which then makes real-time decisions about speed, direction, and braking. This not only makes driving more efficient in terms of its environmental impact but also makes journeys safer. AI allows you to sit back and relax while your car handles the morning commute, choosing the most efficient route, and avoiding traffic jams. And yes, this convenience considerably cuts down on pollution. Self-driving cars can drive more smoothly than humans by avoiding unnecessary acceleration and braking, which means they use less fuel and emit fewer pollutants.

In cities, AI is being used to manage traffic and reduce congestion. Smart traffic systems analyze data from cameras and sensors to suggest the best routes and adjust traffic lights. This means less time stuck in traffic and lower emissions from idling cars. For example, AI can adjust the timing of traffic lights based on the current flow of traffic so cars spend less time idling at red lights and more time moving. These systems can also provide real-time updates to drivers about the best routes to take, which spreads out traffic and reduces bottlenecks.

Public transportation is also getting smarter with AI. Buses and trains can use AI to run their routes and schedules more optimally by following passenger demand. Optimal public transport means more efficient use of public resources and shorter wait times for riders. Imagine a bus route that changes dynamically throughout the day to pick up more passengers during rush hour and save fuel when demand is lower. It makes public transportation more reliable and convenient, encouraging more people to leave their cars at home and use greener options.

Bike-sharing programs are benefiting from AI, too. In many cities, AI monitors bike availability and predicts where bikes will be needed most. Thus, bikes are always available in popular spots. If you've ever used a bike-sharing service, you know how frustrating it can be to find an empty dock. AI helps solve this problem by predicting usage patterns and moving bikes around accordingly.

AI also plays a role in making deliveries more eco-friendly. Companies like Amazon are experimenting with AI-powered delivery drones that can deliver packages quickly while saving natural resources. These drones use AI to navigate and avoid obstacles to bring packages to their destinations safely. By using drones instead of delivery trucks, delivery and mail services can reduce their carbon footprint and make deliveries faster, which is a win-win for the environment and for the people increasingly eager to shop online.

Even parking is getting a tech upgrade thanks to AI. Smart parking systems help drivers find available spots quickly, reducing the time spent circling the block looking for a place to park. These systems use sensors and AI to monitor parking lots and street parking, guiding drivers to the nearest available spot. Parking tech saves time and reduces frustration while also cutting down on emissions from cars driving around aimlessly just to find a parking spot (that may get snatched right before their eyes).

IMAGINING THE FUTURE

Imagining the future of AI is like looking into a cool crystal ball but a little more realistic. AI is changing so fast that it might be hard to keep up, but it is also exciting to think about where it might take us in the next few years.

First off, think about healthcare. AI could completely change how we diagnose and treat diseases. In the future, you might be getting a quick and accurate diagnosis from an AI just by describing your symptoms through an app. AI can analyze medical data to find the best treatments for each person, making personalized medicine the norm. Doctors might even use AI to predict health issues before they become serious. Of course, you'll still want a human doctor on the other side, as no amount of artificial neural networks can replace a knowledgeable human. But it may make the doctor's job much easier and less stressful.

Education could see some big changes, too, and there are already some clear signs. AI tutors could teach in a way that's personal to each student, adapting lessons to fit each child's (or adult's) learning style and pace. This could make learning more effective and fun for everyone. Imagine having an AI tutor that knows exactly what you need help with and gives you extra practice, or one that makes learning games tailored just for you.

In the workplace, AI will likely handle more of the boring, repetitive tasks, freeing up more of your time to focus on more creative and strategic work. It could even eventually lead to that long-sought-after, elusive shorter work day or work week. Imagine AI assistants who help you manage your schedule, sort through emails, and handle some basic decision-making. This could make work more interesting and satisfying. It might also lead to new types of jobs that we can't even imagine yet. Of course, as some rightfully worry, it may displace some positions, but just like with any new technology, it will be a balancing act.

Beyond just setting reminders and answering questions, future AI assistants could manage entire aspects of your life, like planning vacations or managing finances, a bit like a personal secretary. They could learn your preferences over time and make suggestions that fit perfectly with your tastes and habits.

At home, your fridge could keep track of what's inside and suggest recipes or even order groceries when you're running low. Your oven could use sensors to cook food perfectly every time, like a personal chef that makes every meal turn out great.

Home automation could get even smarter. Future AI systems might be able to monitor and maintain your entire house, from cleaning to security. Imagine a home that can detect when something needs repairing and schedule maintenance automatically or a security system that can tell the difference between family members and strangers and send alerts when necessary.

AI could also change how we interact with our environment. Smart cities powered by AI could have a hand in everything from traffic flow to energy use. An AI-powered city of the future could be a city where traffic jams are a thing of the past because AI manages the flow of vehicles or where energy use is so efficient that waste is minimal. These changes could make our cities cleaner, greener, and more livable. It could also make them more organized and safer, as AI has the potential to reduce crime.

AI could impact transportation beyond just cars. Think about AI-powered public transport systems that are incredibly efficient and always on time. Hyperloops and smart trains that adjust speeds and routes based on passenger flow, or even autonomous ships and aircraft that optimize routes for fuel efficiency and safety.

In the creative arts, AI could be a collaborator for artists, musicians, and writers. Artists of the future may be composing music alongside an AI that suggests melodies or writing a book with an AI that helps develop characters and plot twists while also adapting perfectly to the author's style, vision, ideas, themes, and so on. This doesn't mean replacing human creativity but rather enhancing it by providing new ideas and possibilities.

Then there's entertainment. We could eventually see movies and music generated by AI. You could be watching a movie that's exactly what you've always wanted to see, with a storyline and characters straight from your imagination, without you having to be a professional (or even an amateur) filmmaker. Or you could listen to music composed by an AI that knows your favorite genres and artists.

Communication could also get a lot easier. AI might break down language barriers with real-time translation tools that are way better than what we have now. Imagine traveling anywhere in the world and being able to chat with anyone, thanks to your AI translator. This could open up many opportunities for cultural exchange and understanding.

Virtual companions and social robots could provide company and support, especially for the elderly or those living alone. These AI companions could engage in conversations, play games, and help with daily tasks, making life a bit less lonely and more engaging. That doesn't mean replacing genuine human interactions (this has the potential to become unhealthy, no matter how seemingly smart the AI may be), but on the plus side, sometimes talking to something that isn't truly "alive" can be a great help.

AI could potentially even help in mental health too. Virtual therapists powered by AI could offer support and guidance 24/7. You could have an always-ready, non-judgmental ear to hear you vent and suggest coping strategies. While AI systems in mental health wouldn't replace human therapists, they could be a valuable extra, especially for people who might not have easy access to mental health services.

Let's move on to something that feels futuristic but is just as realistic—space exploration. AI-powered robots could one day be visiting distant planets to gather data and perform tasks that are too dangerous or impractical for humans. These robots could make decisions based on what they find, helping us explore space more efficiently. AI might help us uncover the mysteries of the universe.

Looking even further ahead, we might eventually see genuine artificial intelligence—AI that can think and learn like humans, with the potential to be even smarter than we are. Sure, it may presently seem like just science fiction fantasy, but it could happen. It could open up possibilities we can barely imagine today, from solving complex global challenges to exploring the universe. It's both thrilling and a bit unnerving to think about the potential, and it means we need to be thoughtful about how we develop and use these powerful technologies.

As we think about all these possibilities, it's clear that the future of AI is something we will shape until it becomes able to shape itself. The choices made at present about how we develop and use AI will have long-lasting impacts.

Of course, with all these advancements, we have to think about the societal impacts of AI. There are big questions about privacy, job displacement, and the ethical use of AI that we'll need to address. As AI becomes more integrated into our lives, we'll need to make sure it's used in ways that are fair and beneficial rather than controlling, intrusive, discriminatory, suppressive, or just creepy.

CONCLUSION

WHY DO YOU NEED AI IN YOUR LIFE?

Let's take a moment to look back at some of the points we've covered throughout this book. First, we learned what AI actually is and how it works. From machine learning to neural networks, we broke down these complex concepts into bite-sized, understandable pieces.

Then, we explored how AI is already a part of almost everyone's daily life, often in ways they might not even realize, from smart assistants like Alexa and Siri helping with reminders and directions to recommendation algorithms on Netflix and Spotify suggesting what to watch or listen to next. AI is everywhere, sometimes in obvious ways, other times much more subtly.

Then, we moved on to how AI can boost productivity and creativity at work. We saw how tools like Grammarly and AI-driven data analysis platforms save time and improve the work. We also talked about AI in creative fields, like generating art or music, which shows that AI can already do so much more than crunch numbers—it can be a source of inspiration, too.

We also tackled some common misconceptions about AI, like the fear that it will take all jobs and make humans (especially those in office or creative fields) obsolete. As we discovered, AI is more likely to change the nature of work rather than replace it completely, which means both losses and new opportunities in the process. And, of course, we touched on the importance of ethics in AI, making sure that as this technology grows, it does so in a way that's fair and unbiased.

In the hands-on chapters, we got practical. From setting up automated alert systems for emails and notifications using platforms like Zapier to building simple chatbots with Chatfuel, we explored hands-on, real-world ways to incorporate AI into your daily routines. You might've even learned a bit about how to train your own AI models using tools like Google's Teachable Machine, showing that you don't need to be a tech guru to get involved with AI.

Hopefully, all this insight has made AI a little more accessible to you and has shown you how it can make everyday tasks easier and more efficient by improving how you manage your time, helping with creative projects, or just making life a bit more convenient.

STAY CURIOUS, ALWAYS

With artificial intelligence, curiosity truly is the name of the game. Think of AI as an endless playground. There are so many areas to explore, from creating your own projects to seeing how AI is being used in cutting-edge research. Whether you're interested in developing smarter home gadgets, data science, or tinkering with fun AI apps, there's a whole world of possibilities waiting for you as long as you give it a chance.

One of the best ways to stay in touch with the tech and stay in the zone is to keep up with the latest AI news and trends. Follow AI experts and tech blogs, join online forums like Reddit or Stack Overflow, and maybe subscribe to a few AI podcasts. These are all great sources of inspiration and will keep you informed about the newest developments.

Online courses are another fantastic way to deepen your understanding. Coursera, Udemy, Zenva, Khan Academy, and other online learning platforms offer a plethora of AI courses for all levels, whether you're a beginner looking to get a handle on the basics or have more advanced skills and are wanting to learn specific areas like neural networks or natural language processing. Whatever your interests, there's something out there for you.

Never be afraid to get hands-on with AI projects. Start small and work your way up. Maybe begin with some of the practical exercises we discussed, like building a chatbot or training a simple AI model.

As you get more comfortable, you can tackle more complex projects. There are tons of tutorials and community support to help you along the way.

And if you're feeling social, consider joining an AI meetup group or attending AI conferences and workshops. These are great places to meet like-minded people, share ideas, and maybe even collaborate on projects. The AI community is welcoming and open to everyone, with no judgment, and there's always something new to learn from each other.

NEVER STOP LEARNING

AI technology is advancing so quickly that what's cutting-edge today might be old news tomorrow. To really leverage the benefits of AI, keep learning and stay up-to-date. Never give up. This doesn't mean you need dense textbooks or to enroll in a full-time course (unless you want to). Rather, there are plenty of fun and accessible ways to stay in the loop without overwhelming yourself. Even a few minutes of reading an article on what's hot in AI while you sit with your morning coffee could be enough to keep you up-to-date and take little effort.

Follow AI news and trends online to keep on top of the latest innovations. Websites like TechCrunch, Wired, and AI-specific blogs can give you a steady stream of updates. Social media is also a goldmine for the latest in AI—follow tech influencers and join AI discussion groups on Discord, Facebook, Twitter, LinkedIn, or Reddit.

Online courses and tutorials are fantastic resources for continuous learning. Courses range from beginner to advanced levels, ensuring you'll never be truly overwhelmed. Many of these courses are self-paced, so you can learn at your own speed and fit it into your schedule whenever you have the time, even if it takes you months. It's better to learn at your own tempo than rush and become discouraged.

Participating in online forums and communities can also be incredibly helpful. Stack Overflow, GitHub, and various AI subreddits are great places to ask questions (though you might have better luck on Stack Overflow if your knowledge level is a bit more advanced), share knowledge, and learn from others who are just as passionate about AI. You'll find that the AI community is pretty welcoming and ready to help out, and you might end up making a few friends along the way.

Books and podcasts are another great way to keep up. There are tons of engaging AI books that break down complex topics into understandable chunks. Podcasts, on the other hand, are perfect for learning on the go, like when commuting, exercising, or doing chores. You can tune into an AI podcast and absorb new information without carving out extra time in your day.

Workshops, webinars, and conferences also let you learn to no end. These events often feature experts in the field who share their insights and the latest research. They're also a great opportunity to network with others who are as interested in AI as you are, which can lead to exciting collaborations and projects.

The trick to never stop learning is to make learning a regular part of your routine. It doesn't have to be a huge time commitment—just staying curious and dedicating a little time each week to explore new topics can make a big difference. By keeping up with the latest advancements, you'll be better equipped to take advantage of AI's benefits and apply them in ways that make your personal and professional life a little better. So, keep the curiosity alive, stay informed, and enjoy the ride.

THANK YOU!

Thanks a lot for sticking through this book. Hopefully, you have found it both informative and enjoyable. AI is such a fascinating topic, and there's so much more to explore and learn.

If you enjoyed reading this, why not take a few minutes to leave a review? Your feedback helps other readers find this book and motivates the author to keep writing and sharing more about AI and other interesting topics.

But more importantly, don't stop here. Keep exploring AI, try out some of the projects you've learned about here, and stay curious. Join online communities, take courses, follow the latest AI news, and keep finding eye-catching books that spark your interest and curiosity. There's always something new and exciting happening in the world of AI, and you don't want to miss out.

Feel free to share what you've learned with friends and family. Maybe even work on a project together. The more you learn and share, the better you can harness AI to make life easier and more fun.

GLOSSARY

1. ALGORITHM

An algorithm is a set of instructions that tells a computer how to perform a task. Like a recipe, it's a step-by-step guide that takes you from the ingredients (input data) to the finished dish (output). In the context of AI, algorithms help computers learn from data and make decisions rather than strictly control the output, as they would in traditional computing.

2. ARTIFICIAL INTELLIGENCE (AI)

Artificial Intelligence, or AI, is the field of computer science that focuses on creating machines capable of performing tasks that would otherwise require human intelligence. AI includes aspects like understanding natural language, recognizing images, solving problems, and learning from experience. AI is giving machines a figurative brain to think and learn.

3. AUGMENTED REALITY (AR)

Augmented Reality, or AR, is a technology that overlays digital information, like images or sounds, onto the real world. Pokémon Go is one of the best-known examples of AR, where you see Pokémon characters on your phone as if they're there in the real world. AR enhances your perception of reality with computer-generated elements, making things more interactive and fun.

4. AUTOENCODER

An autoencoder is a type of neural network used to learn efficient representations of data, usually for the purpose of dimensionality reduction or feature learning. Think of it as a way for the AI to compress and then decompress data, kind of like how a zip file works. It learns to encode data in a compact form and then reconstruct it as closely as possible to the original input. An autoencoder is super useful for things like image compression or noise reduction.

5. AUTONOMOUS VEHICLES

Autonomous vehicles are self-driving cars and trucks that can navigate and operate without human intervention. These vehicles use a combination of sensors, cameras, radar, and AI to understand their environment, make decisions, and drive safely. However, they usually still require oversight: most vehicles have a self-driving option as an extra alongside the human driver, while fully automated vehicles rely on built-in human directions to make split-second decisions.

6. BACKPROPAGATION

Backpropagation is a method used in training neural networks, which are a type of AI model. It's a feedback loop that helps the network learn by correcting its mistakes. When the network makes a wrong prediction, backpropagation adjusts the network's parameters to reduce the error, like a coach helping an athlete improve by pointing out what went wrong and how to fix it.

7. BAYESIAN NETWORK

A Bayesian Network is a graphical model that represents the probabilistic relationships among a set of variables, such as a map that shows how different events are connected and how likely they are to affect each other. It's a more advanced and interconnected flowchart that helps in understanding the likelihood of various outcomes based on different conditions. It is often used in risk analysis and decision-making.

8. BIAS

Bias in AI refers to the systematic error that can occur in machine learning models when the data used to train the model is not representative of the real world. Think of it like a skewed perspective or a one-sided story. If the training data has biases, the AI model will likely reproduce those biases, leading to unfair or inaccurate predictions. Bias is a big concern in AI ethics because it can result in discrimination or unfair treatment.

9. BIG DATA

Big Data refers to extremely large sets of data that are too complex to handle with traditional data-processing software. Think of it like having a massive library of books, videos, and documents that you need to analyze to find patterns and insights. With the right tools and techniques, Big Data helps organizations, individuals, and researchers make better decisions and discover new trends.

10. CHATBOT

A chatbot is a computer program (often but not always AI-powered) that can simulate conversation with human users, often through messaging apps, websites, or mobile apps. Often, it can come in the form of a virtual assistant that can answer your questions, help you with tasks, or provide customer support—all without needing a human on the other end.

11. CLASSIFICATION

Classification in AI is the categorization of data into predefined groups or classes. For example, you may have a collection of emails that you want to sort into "spam" and "not spam". Classification algorithms can help by learning from examples and then predicting which category new emails belong to.

12. CLUSTERING

Clustering is a technique used to group similar data points together based on their characteristics. It's like sorting a pile of mixed fruits into separate baskets for apples, oranges, and bananas. When data is in clusters, it becomes easier to identify patterns and structures in the data.

13. COLLABORATIVE FILTERING

Collaborative filtering is a method used by recommendation systems to predict what you might like based on the preferences of other users. Imagine you're trying to find a new movie to watch. Collaborative filtering looks at the movies that people with similar tastes to yours have liked and recommends those to you. It's the tech behind recommendations on platforms like Netflix and Amazon.

14. COMPUTER VISION

Computer Vision is a field of AI that enables computers to interpret and understand visual information from the world, just like humans do. It involves teaching machines to recognize objects, faces, and scenes in images or videos. Think about how social media or your phone can automatically tag people in photos or how self-driving cars recognize stop signs and pedestrians—those are all examples of computer vision in action.

15. CONVOLUTIONAL NEURAL NETWORK (CNN)

A convolutional neural network, or CNN, is a type of neural network specifically for processing structured grid data like images. Think of it as a smart filter that can detect patterns and features in pictures, such as edges, textures, or complex shapes like faces. CNNs are widely used in applications like image recognition and computer vision.

16. DATA AUGMENTATION

Data augmentation involves creating new training examples by modifying existing data. Think of it like taking a photo and making several copies with different filters, rotations, or crops to give the AI more examples to learn from. This technique is often used in image processing to help improve the performance of machine learning models by providing them with more varied data.

17. DATA MINING

Data mining is like digging through large amounts of data to find useful patterns, trends, precedents, or insights. Data mining for insights uncovers valuable information that can help you and others (whether individuals or organizations) make better decisions, predict trends, or understand customer behavior.

18. DATA SCIENCE

Data science is the field that involves using statistical methods, algorithms, and technology to analyze and interpret complex data. Data scientists use data to uncover hidden patterns, make predictions, and solve problems. Data scientists often work with big data through data mining to help companies and researchers understand trends and make informed decisions.

19. DATA SET

A data set is simply a collection of data. It could be anything from a list of numbers to a massive table of information. Think of it as a spreadsheet where each row is a different data point, and each column is a different attribute or characteristic. Data sets are the raw material that data scientists and AI algorithms use to learn and make predictions.

20. DECISION TREE

A decision tree is a flowchart-like model used to make decisions using a series of questions or conditions. Imagine you're trying to decide what to eat for dinner, and you create a series of yes/no questions to narrow down your options, like "Do I want something healthy?" or "Do I have the ingredients at home?" Each answer leads you to the next question until you reach a decision. In AI, decision trees classify data and make predictions based on similar logic.

21. DIMENSIONALITY REDUCTION

Dimensionality reduction simplifies your data without losing too much important information. Think of it as decluttering your room—you get rid of stuff you don't need but keep all the essentials. In AI, this means reducing the number of variables or features in a data set to make it easier to analyze and visualize while still preserving the important patterns.

22. DEEP LEARNING

Deep learning is a subset of machine learning that uses neural networks with many layers (hence "deep") to analyze data. Deep Learning teaches a computer to think and learn in a way that's inspired by the human brain. Deep learning has the potential to be better than humans at handling complex tasks like recognizing speech, understanding images, and playing brain-teasing games.

23. DEEPFAKE

A deepfake is a type of synthetic media where AI is used to create realistic but fake images, videos, or audio recordings. Imagine swapping faces in a video so it looks like someone else is speaking or doing something they never actually did. While deepfakes can be fun for making memes or movie effects, they also raise concerns about misinformation and privacy.

24. EDGE COMPUTING

Edge computing is like having a mini data center right where you need it, close to the devices that generate data. Instead of sending all your data to a centralized cloud server, edge computing processes it locally. This speeds things up and reduces the load on your network. It's great for applications where you need quick responses, like in self-driving cars or smart home devices.

25. ETHICS IN AI

Ethics in AI is a field of research and philosophy that explores the use of AI in ways that are fair, transparent, and respectful of people's rights. It involves thinking about the impact of AI on society, avoiding bias in algorithms, protecting people's privacy, and ensuring that AI benefits everyone, not just a select few. While philosophical in nature, the ethics in AI encompasses academic areas such as logic, psychology, ethics, neurology, and more.

26. ENSEMBLE LEARNING

Ensemble learning is a technique where multiple machine learning models are combined to solve a problem. Think of it like getting a second (or third, or fourth) opinion on a tricky question. By using several models together, you can often get more accurate and reliable results than you would with just one model. It's like having a team of experts working on the same task.

27. FEATURE EXTRACTION

Feature extraction is the process of identifying the most important parts of data to make analysis easier and more effective. Imagine you're trying to figure out which ingredients make a recipe taste great. Feature extraction is like picking out those ingredients so you can focus on them above the more complementary ones. In AI, feature extraction means selecting the data's relevant attributes to improve the performance of your models.

28. FEDERATED LEARNING

Federated learning is a way to train machine learning models across multiple devices without sharing the actual data. Imagine all the smartphones learning to predict text without sending your private messages to a central server. Each device learns from its own data, and only the learning updates are shared. Federated learning is a privacy-friendly way to make smarter models.

29. GENETIC ALGORITHM

A genetic algorithm is an optimization technique inspired by the process of natural selection. This inspiration makes it akin to breeding plants or animals to get the best traits, but in this case, you're using it to find the best solution to a problem. The algorithm creates a population of possible solutions and then combines and mutates them over generations to find the most optimal one.

30. GENERATIVE PRE-TRAINED TRANSFORMER (GPT)

Generative pre-trained transformers, or GPTs, are a type of AI model used for natural language processing tasks. Imagine a really smart text generator that can write essays, answer questions, and even create poetry. GPT models are trained on huge amounts of text data and can generate human-like text based on the input they receive. They're behind some of the most advanced chatbots and language models out there.

31. GRADIENT DESCENT

Gradient descent is an optimization algorithm used to minimize the error in machine learning models. Imagine you're hiking down a mountain, and you want to find the lowest point. Gradient descent is like taking small steps downhill, adjusting your path based on the slope until you reach the bottom. It helps models learn by gradually reducing their mistakes.

32. HEURISTICS

Heuristics are simple, rule-of-thumb strategies or principles used to make decisions and solve problems quickly. Think of it as a shortcut your brain uses to come up with a good enough solution without having to think too hard. In AI, heuristics help models make fast decisions when there's no time or need for perfect accuracy.

33. HYPERPARAMETER

A hyperparameter is a setting that you configure before training a machine learning model. For example, when setting the dials on a washing machine before you start a load of laundry or choosing cooking settings on a microwave, you adjust them based on what you're washing or cooking to get the best results. In AI, tuning hyperparameters improves the model's performance and accuracy.

34. HYPERPARAMETER TUNING

Hyperparameter tuning is like finding the perfect settings on your coffee machine to make the best cup of coffee. In AI, hyperparameters are the settings that control how a machine learning model is trained. Tuning these settings can make a big difference in how well your model performs. It's all about tweaking things like learning rates and batch sizes to get the best results.

35. IMAGE CLASSIFICATION

Image classification is the task of assigning a label or category to an image based on its content. If you have a bunch of photos and you want to sort them into groups like "cats", "dogs", and "birds", image classification is the AI's way of recognizing what's in each photo and sorting them into the right categories. It's used in everything from sorting your photo library to helping autonomous cars recognize road signs.

36. IMAGE SEGMENTATION

Image segmentation is a process where an image is divided into different segments or regions, usually to identify and analyze specific parts of the image. Think of it like cutting out pieces of a puzzle where each piece represents a different object or area in the picture. This technique is used in medical imaging, object detection, and computer vision tasks to understand and interpret images more effectively.

37. INTERNET OF BEHAVIOR (IOB)

The Internet of Behavior (IoB) is an extension of the Internet of Things (IoT) that focuses on understanding and influencing human behavior through data collected by IoT devices. Imagine your smartwatch not only tracking your steps but also suggesting healthier habits based on your activity patterns. IoB aims to use this data to create more personalized and effective ways to improve our daily lives.

38. INTERNET OF THINGS (IOT)

The Internet of Things, or IoT, refers to the network of physical devices within a home (or office, etc.) connected to each other and/or the Internet, all collecting and sharing data. Think about smart home gadgets like thermostats, lights, smart power outlets, network storage,

TVs, and refrigerators that you can control with your phone. IoT makes it possible for these devices to communicate with each other and with the user.

39. K-NEAREST NEIGHBORS (KNN)

K-Nearest Neighbors, or KNN, is a simple machine learning algorithm for classification and regression. Imagine you're trying to decide which movie to watch and want AI to lend a hand. KNN helps by finding similar movies that others with similar tastes have liked. It looks at the "nearest neighbors" of a data point (like a movie) and makes predictions based on the preferences of those neighbors.

40. MACHINE LEARNING

Machine learning is a branch of AI where computers learn from data and improve their performance over time without being explicitly programmed. It's like teaching a dog new tricks: you show it what to do, and with enough practice, it gets better at it. Machine learning powers everything from recommendation systems on Netflix to voice assistants like Siri.

41. NATURAL LANGUAGE PROCESSING (NLP)

Natural language processing, or NLP, is a field of AI that enables computers to understand and interact with human language. Natural language processing effectively teaches a computer to speak and understand English or any other language. NLP is behind technologies like chatbots, translation services, and voice recognition systems, making it possible for us to communicate with machines in a natural way rather than through strict commands (as traditional programs might demand).

42. NEURAL ARCHITECTURE SEARCH (NAS)

Neural architecture search, or NAS, is like having an AI assistant help you design the best neural network for your task. Instead of manually figuring out the best network structure, NAS automates the process, searching for the optimal architecture that delivers the best performance. It's like having a super-smart assistant who knows all the tricks to build the best model for you.

43. NEURAL NETWORK

A neural network is a type of AI model that somewhat resembles the human brain. It consists of layers of interconnected nodes (or neurons) that work together to process data and make decisions. Think of neural networks as a web of tiny, connected decision-makers that learn from data. Neural networks are used in a variety of applications, from recognizing faces in photos to predicting stock market trends.

44. OVERFITTING

Overfitting happens when a machine learning model learns the training data too well, including the noise and details that don't matter, much like memorizing a textbook word-for-word instead of understanding the main concepts. A model that has been overfitted will perform great on the training data but struggle with new, unseen data because its programming is too specific to the examples it was trained on.

45. PATTERN RECOGNITION

Pattern recognition is the ability of a computer to identify patterns and regularities in data. When being taught pattern recognition, a computer can recognize that a cat is a cat, no matter if it's black, white, or orange. This skill is necessary in many AI applications, like recognizing handwritten text, detecting faces in photos, or spotting trends in financial data.

46. PREDICTIVE ANALYTICS

Predictive analytics involves using data, statistical algorithms, and machine learning techniques to identify the likelihood of future outcomes based on historical data. Predictive analysis helps businesses forecast sales, manage risks, or predict when equipment might fail. Also, predictive analysis can benefit government organizations, researchers, weather forecasts, and engineers, just to name a few.

47. RANDOM FOREST

A random forest is a versatile machine learning algorithm that builds multiple decision trees and merges them together to get a more accurate and stable prediction. Imagine a group of friends voting on a decision, like where to go for dinner. Instead of relying on one person's choice, you make a better decision by considering everyone's input. Similarly, a random forest combines the decisions of multiple trees to improve accuracy and reduce overfitting.

48. RECURRENT NEURAL NETWORK (RNN)

A recurrent neural network, or RNN, is a type of neural network designed to handle sequential data, like time series or sentences. Imagine you're trying to predict the next word in a sentence. RNNs have a memory that helps them remember previous words to make better predictions. They're great for tasks like language translation, speech recognition, and even generating music.

49. REINFORCEMENT LEARNING

Reinforcement learning is a type of machine learning where an agent learns to make decisions by performing actions and receiving feedback. For comparison, think about training a dog (or a cat) with treats: the animal tries different actions, and when it does something right, it gets a treat. Over time, it learns to perform the actions that earn the most treats. In AI, this approach is used in applications like game playing, robotics, and autonomous driving.

50. REGRESSION

Regression is a type of machine learning used to predict a continuous outcome based on input data. Think of forecasting the weather as an example: by looking at various factors like temperature, humidity, and wind speed, a regression model can predict tomorrow's temperature. The system must find the relationship between variables to make predictions.

51. ROBOTICS

Robotics is the field of technology focused on designing, building, and operating physical robots, not just virtual AI. Robots can be anything from simple machines that perform repetitive tasks in factories to advanced humanoids that can interact with people. Robotics combines engineering, computer science, and AI to create machines that can help us in various ways, like assembling cars or exploring Mars.

52. SEMI-SUPERVISED LEARNING

Semi-supervised learning is a machine learning approach that uses a mix of labeled and unlabeled data for training. Let's imagine you're learning to play the piano with a few lessons (labeled data) and then practice on your own (unlabeled data). The self-guided practice instills the knowledge more deeply. This method improves learning efficiency when labeled data is scarce or expensive to obtain.

53. SENTIMENT ANALYSIS

Sentiment analysis is the process of using AI to determine the emotional tone behind a piece of text. The AI-equipped computer learns to understand whether a review is positive, negative, or neutral. Companies might use sentiment analysis to gauge customer opinions on products, services, or marketing campaigns by analyzing reviews, social media posts, and other forms of feedback. Political campaigners might use it to determine the overall public opinion on certain policies, and so on.

54. SUPERVISED LEARNING

Supervised learning is a type of machine learning where the model is trained using labeled data. The data comes with the correct answers (labels), and the model learns to make predictions based on that information. For example, you could train a supervised learning model to recognize spam emails by feeding it examples of both spam and non-spam emails.

55. SUPPORT VECTOR MACHINE (SVM)

Support vector machine, or SVM, is a type of machine learning algorithm for classification and regression tasks. Imagine you're trying to separate different types of fruit on a table. SVM draws the best possible line (or boundary) between them depending on their features, like color or size, so that you can easily classify any new fruit that comes along. The machine acts the same, trying to find the optimal way to separate data points into different groups.

56. SUPPORT VECTOR REGRESSION (SVR)

Support vector regression, or SVR, is a cousin of SVM but is used for regression tasks instead of classification. Think of it as trying to predict a continuous value, like the price of a house, based on different features. SVR finds the best line (or curve) that fits the data points, helping you make accurate predictions about new, unseen data.

57. TENSORFLOW

TensorFlow is an open-source library developed by Google for building and training machine learning models. It is a powerful toolkit that helps developers and researchers create AI applications, whether simple experiments or complex, large-scale projects. It's used for everything from recognizing images to natural language processing.

58. TEACHABLE MACHINE

Teachable Machine is the name of a user-friendly web tool by Google that lets you train your own machine learning models without needing to write any code. Instead, you play with a fun, interactive app where you can teach the computer to recognize images, sounds, or poses by showing it examples. It's a great way for beginners with little to no coding knowledge to get hands-on experience with AI.

59. TEST DATA

Test data is the data set used to evaluate the performance of a machine learning model after it has been trained. Think of it as a final exam for the model. You've already taught it (trained it) using one set of data, and now you're seeing how well it can apply what it learned to new, unseen data. Test data determines how well the model generalizes to real-world scenarios.

60. TRAINING DATA

Training data is the data set that has been used when teaching a machine learning model. It gives the model a vast amount of practice problems to learn from. Each example in the training data includes the input features and the correct output so the model can learn the relationship between them. The better and more comprehensive the training data, the better the model can perform on new tasks.

61. TRANSFER LEARNING

Transfer learning is a technique in machine learning where a model trained on one task can adapt to working on a different but related task. Imagine you're really good at playing the guitar, and because of that, you can quickly pick up playing the ukulele. With regard to AI, this means using an existing model trained on a large dataset to solve a new problem with less data and time.

62. TURING TEST

The Turing Test, proposed by Alan Turing, is a way to determine if a machine can exhibit intelligent behavior indistinguishable from that of a human. Carrying out the Turing Test could mean having a conversation with a chatbot and trying to figure out if you're talking to a human or a machine. If you can't tell the difference, the AI passes the test.

63. UNSUPERVISED LEARNING

Unsupervised learning is a type of machine learning where the model is trained using data that doesn't have labeled outcomes, like exploring a new city without a map and finding patterns or landmarks on your own. For the AI, this means the model looks for patterns and structures in the data without being told what to look for, such as grouping similar items together (clustering) or identifying hidden patterns.

64. VIRTUAL REALITY (VR)

Virtual reality, or VR, is a technology that immerses you in a completely virtual environment using a headset and sometimes additional equipment like gloves or controllers. With VR, you step into a video game or a 3D simulation where you can look around and interact with things as if you were there. VR is used for gaming, training, education, and even virtual travel.

65. VOICE RECOGNITION

Voice recognition is a technology that lets computers understand and process human speech by listening to it. It means talking to your computer, phone, or smart speaker and having it understand your commands, like asking for the weather, playing a song, or setting a reminder. Voice recognition powers virtual assistants like Siri, Alexa, and Google Assistant and also works on Windows and other operating systems, making it easier to interact with technology using just your voice.

66. WEAK AI

Weak AI, also known as Narrow AI, refers to AI systems that can perform a specific task or a limited range of tasks and not much else. Unlike human intelligence, which is general and adaptable, weak AI is really good at one thing. For example, a chess-playing AI can beat grandmasters at chess, but it can't drive a car or hold a conversation. It's a super-specialized tool that excels in its particular job but doesn't have a broader understanding or consciousness.

67. WEIGHTS

Weights are key components in neural networks and other machine learning models. They're like the adjustable dials or knobs that the model tunes during training to make accurate predictions. In a neural network, weights determine the strength of the connection between neurons. By adjusting these weights, the model learns from the data and improves its accuracy over time.

68. XAVIER INITIALIZATION

Related to weights, Xavier initialization is a technique that can set the initial weights of a neural network before training begins. It's named after Xavier Glorot, one of the researchers who proposed it. This method helps start the training on the right foot by preventing the network's outputs from becoming too large or too small. You can consider it as giving the model a balanced starting point so it can learn more effectively.

69. XGBOOST

XGBoost stands for extreme gradient boosting, a powerful machine learning algorithm great for structured or tabular data. It's a turbocharged version of traditional boosting algorithms but boasts an almost unparalleled speed and performance. XGBoost builds multiple decision trees and combines them to produce a highly accurate model. All this makes it popular in data science competitions and practical applications like fraud detection and recommendation systems.

70. ZERO-SHOT LEARNING

Zero-shot learning is a type of machine learning where the model can recognize and classify objects it has never seen before. It's like a person being able to identify a new animal species (or at least determine that it is an animal) based on descriptions or features they've learned about other animals. In AI, zero-shot learning uses knowledge from related tasks to make predictions about new tasks without needing additional training data for those specific tasks. Zero-shot learning helps AI systems generalize and adapt to new challenges more effectively.

Made in the USA
Monee, IL
01 February 2025

11381166R00095